POPULAR WOODWORKING BOOKS
CINCINNATI, OHIO
www.popularwoodworking.com

READ THIS IMPORTANT SAFETY NOTICE

To prevent accidents, keep safety in mind while you work. Use the safety guards installed on power equipment; they are for your protection. When working on power equipment, keep fingers away from saw blades, wear safety goggles to prevent injuries from flying wood chips and sawdust, wear headphones to protect your hearing, and consider installing a dust vacuum to reduce the amount of airborne sawdust in your woodshop. Don't wear loose clothing, such as neckties or shirts with loose sleeves, or jewelry, such as rings, necklaces or bracelets, when working on power equipment. Tie back long hair to prevent it from getting caught in your equipment. People who are sensitive to certain chemicals should check the chemical content of any product before using it. The authors and editors who compiled this book have tried to make the contents as accurate and correct as possible. Plans, illustrations, photographs and text have been carefully checked. All instructions, plans and projects should be carefully read, studied and understood before beginning construction. Due to the variability of local conditions, construction materials, skill levels, etc., neither the author nor Popular Woodworking Books assumes any responsibility for any accidents, injuries, damages or other losses incurred resulting from the material presented in this book. Prices listed for supplies and equipment were current at the time of publication and are subject to change. Glass shelving should have all edges polished and must be tempered. Untempered glass shelves may shatter and can cause serious bodily injury. Tempered shelves are very strong and if they break will just crumble, minimizing personal injury.

Metric Conversion Chart

to convert	*to*	*multiply by*
Inches	Centimeters	2.54
Centimeters	Inches	0.4
Feet	Centimeters	30.5
Centimeters	Feet	0.03
Yards	Meters	0.9
Meters	Yards	1.1

Published by Popular Woodworking Books, an imprint of F+W Publications, Inc., 4700 East Galbraith Road, Cincinnati, Ohio, 45236. First edition.

Distributed in Canada by Fraser Direct
100 Armstrong Avenue
Georgetown, Ontario L7G 5S4
Canada

Distributed in the U.K. and Europe by David & Charles
Brunel House
Newton Abbot
Devon TQ12 4PU
England
Tel: (+44) 1626 323200
Fax: (+44) 1626 323319
E-mail: postmaster@davidandcharles.co.uk

Distributed in Australia by Capricorn Link
P.O. Box 704
Windsor, NSW 2756
Australia

Visit our Web site at www.popularwoodworking.com or our consumer Web site at www.fwbookstore.com for information on more resources for woodworkers and other arts and crafts projects.

Other fine Popular Woodworking Books are available from your local bookstore or direct from the publisher.

11 10 09 08 07 5 4 3 2 1

Library of Congress Cataloging-in-Publication Data

I can do that! Woodworking projects / edited by David Thiel. -- 1st ed.
p. cm.
ISBN-10: 1-55870-816-2 (pbk. : alk. paper)
ISBN-13: 978-1-55870-816-7 (pbk. : alk. paper)

1. Woodwork--Amateurs' manuals. 2. House furnishings. I. Thiel, David, 1962-
TT185.I22 2007
684'.08--dc22
2007009939

ACQUISITIONS EDITOR: David Thiel
EDITOR: David Thiel
DESIGNER: Brian Roeth
PRODUCTION COORDINATOR: Mark Griffin
ILLUSTRATOR: John Hutchinson

FROM THE EDITOR

It was with great pride that I was able to be a part of the *Popular Woodowrking* magazine staff that brought the I Can Do That! concept to life. It gave me even more pleasure to be able to expand the idea into book form as presented here. Special recognition goes to the magazine staff, Christopher Schwarz, Robert Lang and Megan Fitzpatrick, for the initial (and continuing) work on the concept. Extended recognition goes to Dave Griessman, A.J. Hamler and Glen Huey for taking up the task of building new projects, and for accepting the idealogy of turning out quality projects with a minimum of tools and basic home center materials. Thanks also to John Hutchinson for combining some of his past work for the magazine with new material to present all of our illustrations for the projects—a vital part of the successful building process. Thanks, once again, to all.
—*David Thiel*

ABOUT THE AUTHORS

A.J. Hamler
A.J. Hamler is the former editor of *Woodshop News* and was the founding editor of *Woodcraft Magazine*. As a freelance writer, A.J.'s woodworking articles have appeared in most of the publications in the field and he recently served as Senior Editor for *The Collins Complete Woodworker* for HarperCollins/Smithsonian. When not in his workshop, his other interests include science fiction (writing as A.J. Austin he's published two novels and numerous short stories), gourmet cooking and Civil War reenacting. He lives in Williamstown, W.Va.

Megan Fitzpatrick
Megan is managing editor for *Popular Woodworking* and earned a master's degree in English literature from the University of Cincinnati, which enables her to quote large blocks of Shakespeare—mighty handy in a shop setting.

Dave Griessman
Dave builds reproduction furniture in his "free" time and is working towards owning his own furniture making business. Dave lives in Cincinnati, Ohio.

Glen Huey
Glen recently joined the staff of *Popular Woodworking* as senior editor, but has been in the pages as a contributing editor for a number of years. He is the author of a number of books on building furniture. He also teaches and hosts DVDs about furniture building.

Robert Lang
Bob is senior editor with *Popular Woodworking* magazine and grew up in northeastern Ohio and has been a professional woodworker since the early 1970s. He learned woodworking repairing wooden boats at Lake Erie and in a large commercial shop in Cleveland. Along the way he studied industrial design at The Ohio State University, and his experience includes building custom furniture and cabinets as well as managing and engineering large architectural millwork projects. He is the author of several *Shop Drawings* books about furniture and interiors of the Arts & Crafts Movement of the early 1900s.

Christopher Schwarz
Chris is editor of *Popular Woodworking* magazine and is a long-time amateur woodworker and professional journalist. He built his first workbench at age eight and spent weekends helping his father build two houses on the family's farm outside Hackett, Arkansas — using mostly hand tools. He has journalism degrees from Northwestern University and The Ohio State University and worked as a magazine and newspaper journalist before joining *Popular Woodworking* in 1996. Despite his early experience on the farm, Chris remains a hand-tool enthusiast.

TABLE OF CONTENTS

YES YOU CAN DO IT!

When you get started in woodworking there are many paths to follow, forks in the road, dead-ends and shortcuts. It's a journey that our forebears would make with the help of a living, breathing guide: a master, a grandfather, a shop teacher.

Sadly, the guides are fewer in number today. And so you are left with people like me to help. Like the making of meat by-products, it's not a pretty sight. Getting your woodworking instruction from books, magazines, television and the occasional class is a slow way to learn a complex task. In fact, many woodworkers spend a long time (years!) simply accumulating machines and tools before they ever build a single piece of furniture. And when they do begin to build, they inevitably discover that they actually need different machines and tools to make what they really want to make.

So they buy more tools and machines.

I want you to know something important that doesn't get said much: There is another way to begin building furniture. You don't need a table saw, a workbench or even a shop. You don't need to spend $1,000 to build your first birdhouse. You can go to the home center in the morning and start building something the same day.

I'm not talking about building junk, either. The difference between a nice-looking set of bookshelves and a rude

assemblage of 2 × 4s isn't a table saw. The difference is cleverness, sound design and just a wee bit of patience.

To build nice furniture you need a handful of decent tools that you won't outgrow. This book will help you select the right tools that strike a balance between price and function. You need to use these tools correctly; we'll show you how to use them to build furniture (something you rarely find in the instruction manual). You need a place to work; a driveway, garage or corner of the basement will do nicely. You need good materials; we'll show you how to get everything you need from the local home center. And you need plans and ideas for things to build that look nice and can be constructed with these tools, methods and materials.

In every issue of *Popular Woodworking* magazine we publish a column called "I Can Do That" because we want readers to say that (out loud or in their heads) when they read the magazine (and now this book). We started with some of the plans used in the magazine and have added another ten, built specifically for this book and for you.

Eventually, we think you'll outgrow the manual part of this book (and on the web at www.icandothatextras.com) as your skills improve. I bet you will want a table saw someday. And a drill press. And a smoothing plane. When that day comes, however, you'll also have a house full of well-proportioned, well-built projects under your belt. You will be ready for those awesome tools, and the learning curve will be mercifully short.

If all this sounds like something that a bunch of idealists cooked up at a corporate strategy meeting, you're wrong. Though I had some carpentry training from my father and grandfather, I started building furniture on my back porch in Lexington, Kentucky, with a very similar set of tools. Probably the only major difference is that I had a circular saw instead of a miter saw (I didn't know those existed yet). I built a lot of stuff with my simple setup — some stuff we still have today and some stuff that was long ago abandoned at the curb or given away.

So this, dear reader, is a valid path.

My only regret in following it is that I wish I'd had this book (or a master) to make the journey easier.

— Christopher Schwarz, Editor *Popular Woodworking* magazine

RULES FOR USING THE TOOLS

"The pioneers cleared the forests from Jamestown to the Mississippi with fewer tools than are stored in the modern garage."

— unknown, attributed to Dwayne Laws

I'm not an emotional guy. I don't get nostalgic about high school, my first car or my first dog, Scampy. I don't much hug family members at holiday gatherings. But I do have the deepest respect and affection for my tools. The care you give tools will gush readily into the things you build with them. None of the tools in the following kit are disposable; if you take good care of them, they will be around for many years of service.

STOP RUST

Here are some basic tips for caring for all tools. Don't you dare let them rust. Rust spreads like a cancer in ferrous materials (iron and steel) and can make your measuring and cutting tools difficult to use. There are a lot of products out there to prevent and remove rust, but the best thing going cannot be found on the shelf: a small can of vigilance.

When you are done with a tool, wipe down the metal surfaces – especially the cutting surface – with a rag that has been soaked with WD-40. Always keep the rag nearby (mine is seven years old) and renew it with a squirt of WD-40 when it gets dry. Wiping your tool down does two things: First, it removes dust from the tool. Dust can carry salt. Salt attracts water. The combination of salt and moisture will start breaking down your iron and steel tools.

Second, the WD-40 helps prevent rust by forming a thin protective barrier, albeit one that must be constantly renewed to be effective. Other people will disparage WD-40 (I once did). Ignore them. We tested all the rust preventative products on the market one spring weekend. We applied the products to a cast-iron plate and left the plate outside in the dewy grass for a couple of days. The area treated with WD-40 came out of the test looking the best. WD-40 is cheap. It's readily available. It won't stain your work. Spray some on a piece of wood and watch what happens. Once it dries, there's nothing to see.

LEARN TO SEE

All of your tools require tweaking and maintenance. They might work perfectly right out of the box; they might not. It all depends on who made the tool and what sort of day they were having when your tool came down the assembly line — whether the assembler was a robot or a person.

You need to learn to set up your tools so they do what they were intended to do – cut square, bore straight holes, measure accurately. Once you set them up, you need to check on them every once in a while. Trust, but verify. It's a fact: Tools lose their settings after regular use.

In fact, one of the biggest challenges in woodworking is training your eye to see the right things. You need to learn to see if the cut is square. You need to see if your square is square. Have you ever heard the old expression "tried and true?" It is an expression that applies to your tools as well as your work. When you make a cut you should test it to make sure it's the cut you wanted – this is called *trying* your work. If the cut is correct it is said to be *true*. Likewise with your tools, you must try them to ensure they are cutting true. We're going to show you how to test all of your tools (and joints) so they are true. It's not hard, and it pays off big-time.

BUYING QUALITY

You can spend a ridiculous sum on any tool – ridiculously huge and ridiculously small. Jigsaws can cost $35 to $500. Awls can cost $2 to $180. I wouldn't recommend you buy the tool on either extreme of the spectrum. It would be easy for us to say simply: "Buy the best you can afford." But that's a cop-out. If money is tight, you shouldn't buy the $35 jigsaw. You should wait and save a bit more cash. If you're a wealthy heiress, you shouldn't buy the $180 scratch awl just because you can afford it (save your money for some real jewelry).

What's important is to buy tools that do what they are supposed to do. Tools that hold their settings. Tools that are easy to maintain and adjust. Tools that are reasonably durable. Tools that are safe. We are going to explain what is important about each tool, and what is not. We might not be able to offer brand-name advice or model numbers because those change from month to month and from city to city (no lie; ask me about that fact over a beer sometime). But we can help you narrow your choices considerably.

All of the tools on our list can be purchased from a home center or a hardware store. There is no specialty stuff on the list to search the world for.

MEASURING TOOLS

You want to buy both of your measuring tools – a 12" combination square and a 16' tape measure – at the same time so you can check the scale on one to make sure it matches the other. They are unlikely to disagree, but if they do, you'll be chasing your tail for a long time before you figure out what the problem is. To buy these tools, take with you to the store a mechanical pencil and a scrap of wood that is at least 6" square and has one straight edge.

In general, we recommend a metal-bodied combination square. These are, usually, more durable and accurate.

12" COMBINATION SQUARE

This is the tool that will lay out your joints and cuts, and check all your work to ensure your cuts are accurate. The home center should have a few different brands available with some variation in price. Here's what's important:

First, the square must be square. The ruler and head must meet at 90° or the tool is worthless. There are ways to tweak a faulty square, but we don't recommend them. It's not something you should have to do. This is why you brought the wood and the pencil along with you – they will help you sort through the pile of combination squares to find the most accurate one in the bunch. Don't be embarrassed to do this in the store; they should be embarrassed that you have to do this.

First, take the ruler and press one edge against the straight edge of your board to confirm that the edge is straight. Generally you don't want to see any light peeking out between the ruler and the wood. If your wood is out of whack, wander over to the lumber section to look for an offcut to borrow. Usually there's a barrel by the panel saw or radial arm saw where they cut down big stock into small stock for customers.

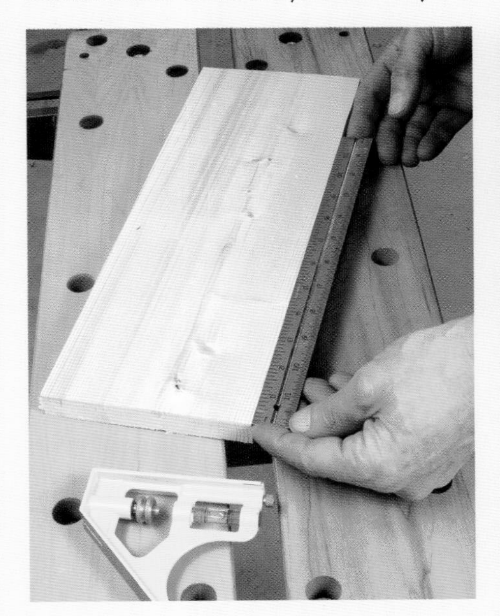

The ruler from your combination square can confirm if the edge of the board is straight. Off-the-rack lumber will usually have at least one decent edge.

Accuracy is important here. Keep the square registered securely against the wood as you scribe the line. If anything feels like it shifted during scribing, make another line. Use a mechanical pencil to ensure your line is consistent in width.

Now flip the square over and show the ruler to the line. If your square is true and your line consistent, then the line and the ruler should be perfectly parallel. If the line and the ruler don't match up, try the operation again before you reject the square – it's easy to trip yourself up when checking your square.

With the square reassembled, press the head of the combination square against the straight edge of the board and use your fingers to hold the ruler down and steady against the face of the board. With a pencil, scribe a thin line along the edge of the ruler. Make it as thin and consistent as possible. If the square moves or the line changes thickness, simply move the square and try again.

Now flip the square over so the other face of the ruler is flat against the face of your board and hold the head of the square against the edge. Push the square up to your perfect line; this is called "showing the line to the square." If the edge of the ruler is perfectly parallel to your pencil line, you have found a square that is indeed square. Congratulations. If the line is slightly off, try the test again. If it's off in the same way, put the square back for another sucker, er – shopper.

Now look at the ruler itself. It must be readable. Look for fine dimension marks. Better-quality squares will have them engraved in the metal rather than printed on. Ideally, you want the ruler to have different scales on each edge. The best combination squares will have one scale in 8ths of an inch, another in 16ths, 32nds and 64ths. You can get away without the 64ths. The 32nds are helpful in most cases. The 16ths are non-negotiable and necessary.

Remove the square from its head by loosening the nut below the ruler. The ruler should be easy to remove and replace. You'll be doing this quite a bit. Now tighten up the nut and make sure the ruler locks firmly in place. It should stay put when you tug on it.

Check out the rest of the square. Is there a bubble level in the head? Yes? No? It doesn't much matter; it's mostly worthless in such a small tool. Is there a removable scribe/scratch awl in the head? Again, pretty worthless in my book. I seem to lose mine right away, but never miss it. It's too small to use anyway.

Treat your combination square like it is a holy relic. If it gets knocked to the floor, curse yourself and then test it immediately. If it's out of true, get in your car and head back to the hardware store. Throw away the old head but keep the ruler – it's still useful. Never slide the ruler needlessly through the head (I've seen some people who do this like it's a nervous tic). This activity wears the area where the head meets the ruler. I've had squares that went out of true after only a couple hundred full-length motions through the head. If that happens to you, buy a better brand of square next time.

16' TAPE MEASURE

First, why not buy a 50' tape measure like all the contractors have on *This Old House*? My dad always mocks my 16' tape measure. "That," he says, "is for girls." Let me tell you, the big tape measures are a pain for furniture work. They curl up more and are hard to lay flat on the work. They weigh a lot. They are bulky. They rarely have the right scales on them.

A 16' tape measure is just the right size for furniture and cabinet work. I sometimes use a 12' tape, but it isn't appreciably smaller or cheaper than the 16' tapes, which are pretty easy to find. The first thing to do when buying a tape measure is to pull the tape out and look at the scale. It's nice to have 16ths on the entire length and 32nds along the first 12" or so.

A 12' or 16' tape measure is a good size for building furniture and dealing with household projects. When you start building houses, then you can step up to the big-boy tapes.

The hook should move in and out. The distance it moves should be equal to the thickness of the hook itself. Tweak the hook with pliers until the tape consistently measures inside and outside measurements.

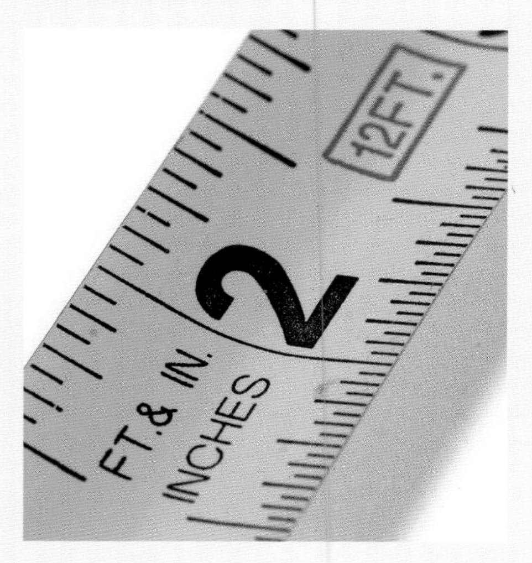

After comparing about 15 brands, I like the Lufkin scales. They have fine graduations and avoid the ridiculous gimmickry on some scales (some measure in 10ths of an inch!). Note the 32nds at the bottom and the 16ths at the top.

Now compare the scale on your combination square with the scale on the tape measure. They should match up. Line them up on the 1" mark and check the dimension lines between 1" and 2". The tape itself is important. You want the lines to be as fine as possible and you want the tape to lay as flat as possible on the work (this makes it easy to mark and measure accurately).

There also is a thing called *standout* with tape measures, this is how far out the tape will extend before it bends and droops. For building furniture, this is not a big deal – a mere 36" to 48" of standout is

Always check your tape measure against your combination square to ensure that the graduations are similarly fine and actually line up. Manufacturers of tape measures and combination squares swear that inaccurate scales cannot occur. I, however, have found occasional discrepancies.

no problem in the shop. (Know, however, that you can never visit a home-building site with this sissy tool.)

Now check the tab, sometimes called the hook, on the end of the tape measure. It should move a little bit. How much? Exactly as much as the thickness of the tip of the hook. If the hook is 1/32" thick, the hook should slide forward and back 1/32". Some people foolishly glue (or weld) the hook so it doesn't move. This prevents you from taking accurate measurements on either the inside or outside of your work. When you measure the inside of a box, the hook is pushed in so the outside face of the hook is zero. When you measure the outside of a piece, the hook is pushed out so that the inside face of the hook is zero.

You can tweak the hook a bit with pliers back at home in order to make the tape measure accurate for inside and outside measurements. For now, find one wheather the hook looks like it moves enough to be accurate.

There are other features on a tape measure that are personal. A clip for the belt is necessary. The locking mechanism should be easy to activate and release – but not too easy. I've always fumbled with the tape measures that release by pressing a plate on the underside of the tool. I constantly retract the tape by mistake. Also – and this might sound funny – I like to have a brightly colored tape measure. The color makes it easy to find when you set it down.

STYLES OF SAWS

We had some long discussions about which kind of portable saws should be in this tool kit. The circular saw seemed a natural part of the tool kit, but it has some limitations when dealing with smaller work, and it won't cut miters that are good enough for picture frames (I'm sure someone can do it; but we can't). Plus, it can be difficult to find saw blades that have enough teeth to make a furniture-grade cut. Circular saws are best suited for the job site.

In the end, we settled on a jigsaw for rip cuts and curves, and a 10" miter saw for crosscuts and miters. The jigsaw has the disadvantage that you need to clean up your rip cuts with a block plane. But its advantages far outweigh that disadvantage. (Plus, learning to use a block plane is an essential furniture-building skill; more on that later). The jigsaw cuts curves beautifully and it is safe, powerful and inexpensive. Plus, with a little practice, you'll find that you need very little clean-up of your sawn edges. We'll show you how to achieve this (the trick is the blade you buy and your left thumb).

The miter saw is a great crosscutting tool for fine and rough work when it is properly tweaked. It will make airtight crosscuts, perfect miters and even break down stock into manageable lengths for you to work with your other tools. A simple 10" miter saw may be limited in capacity to cut only a 1×8, but when you're dealing with off-the-rack lumber from the home center, 1×8 is likely the largest lumber with which you'll be dealing. Let's look at these tools in detail.

This is a barrel-grip jigsaw – chic and European and hard to find in North America. Too bad; some of us really like the lower center of gravity. If you can find a jigsaw like this one at your home center, we recommend it. If you can't – don't worry about it.

JIGSAW

This tool seems so simple, yet it is a subtle thing, capable of immense finesse in skilled hands. There are lots of features on this tool that are rarely discussed from a furniture-making perspective, but that's exactly what we're going to do here.

First, there's the body style of the saw. There are two kinds of bodies: the common top-handle grip and the more European *barrel-grip* style. I absolutely hate to do this to you, but I encourage you to look for the barrel-grip saw. It bewilders me that the top-handle saw is the dominant style in this country. These tools are more tippy and harder to steer than the barrel-grip tools. This tippiness is not a big deal when you're just trying to notch some 2×4s on the job site, but it makes an appreciable difference in the shop. Keeping both your hands and the tool lower to the work improves your control. This maxim is not just for beginners; this applies to everyone.

Here you can see what we're talking about. On the standard top-handle jigsaw, (behind the Festool) your hands will be much higher – 3" to 4" higher. That said, I wouldn't reject either of these jigsaws – both cost more than my monthly truck payment.

The next most important thing is the blade-release mechanism. This is something you're going to be using quite a bit, so it should be simple. The best blade-release mechanisms are almost effortless: Pull a lever and the blade drops out or pops out. Lots of saws have sticky mechanisms – you don't want to have to grab the blade and wiggle it or tug it to remove it from the body. Eventually you will cut yourself.

Older saws need special screwdrivers or require you to twist a knob a good deal to remove the blade. Avoid these if you can

Shown is a properly set jigsaw with the orbital on 1. When you work in thicker material (or need to saw really fast), switch to 2 or 3.

because there are less frustrating ways to work. Speaking of blade-holding mechanisms, there are two dominant styles of blade-holding mechanisms on the market: a T-style and a Universal style or U-style. The T-style blade has a (surprise) T-shaped

Most people don't check the blade to ensure it's square to the baseplate, but it's a good idea. Even the best saws (such as this Bosch) will go out of alignment. If you don't check this occasionally, you'll be in for a rude shock when you try to do some precision work.

shank on top. The Universal-style blade has a hole bored in the blade. I've used both. I don't really have a preference. In fact, my preference is to buy a jigsaw that can hold either style blade. The jigsaw gurus tell me that this compromise results in a blade-holding mechanism that is weak. But I have never had a jigsaw blade come out of the tool while I was working.

Jigsaws have different *strokes,* which is the amount that the blade travels up and down in the tool. A 1" stroke is typical and fine. Shorter-stroke saws are generally at the very low end of the price spectrum and should be avoided anyway. You'll also see a lot of hype about the amperage of a tool. By and large, this is not important for furniture work. I'd give up a couple of amps of alleged power in exchange for a 12' power cord any day. And do check the length of the cord. A short cord will get hung up your work where the plug meets the extension cord.

Another feature that gets played up is the orbital setting. The orbital setting is the amount that the blade will travel back and forth in the cut. Usually, most saws have four settings: zero, one, two and three. Zero means no forward movement,

It's also good to test your results occasionally. If your blade is square to the baseplate but your work isn't square, there could be a couple of problems. You could be cutting too fast, causing your blade to deflect. Or your blade might be slightly bent. Either problem requires a remedy.

With a little practice you'll be able to cut very close to the line with your jigsaw. If you can leave just 1⁄32" of waste, then it's simple work to rasp (or sand) down to your line. If you cross the line while cutting, you'll have no line to rasp to. Make a relief cut into the corner before cutting the curve.

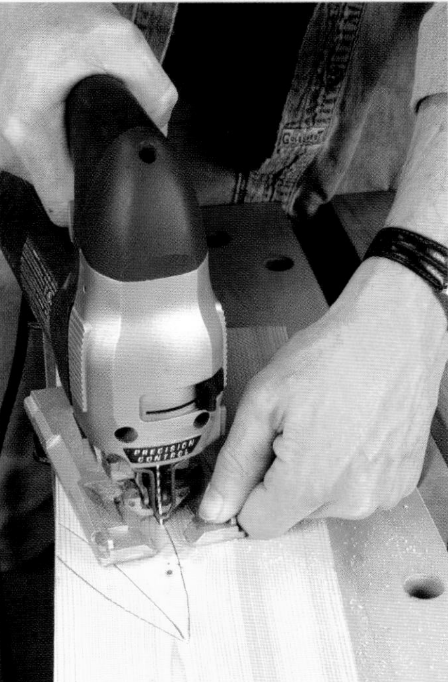

The jigsaw is a two-handed tool. A thumb on the baseplate will help steady the tool and will allow you great finesse as you round curves and track a line. We've removed the plastic guard on this saw for clearer pictures. With the guard in place, it's quite a feat to cut yourself.

which results in a slow cut but a clean one (generally). Three is when you need to cut plywood to cover your windows for an oncoming hurricane. It's fast and rough. Set your saw to one and you'll be fine until you move into the thick stuff.

How about a blower, do you need one? A blower puffs away dust from your cut line to make it easier to follow. I like a blower, otherwise I find myself doing all the puffing and turning blue. How about a worklight? It's not a must-have, but if your saw has one, you'll use it and like it. It can get dark down there by the blade.

Other features aren't so important. How you bevel the base of the saw is pretty irrelevant – some manufacturers play up the fact that the saw requires no tools. I rarely find the need to bevel the base. Once a year maybe. So no big deal. Do make sure that your blade is cutting straight down. You can check this first with your combination square, but keep the ruler away from the teeth of the blade. The teeth can be bent, or set, to either side of the blade on some blades. Register the ruler against the steel behind the teeth.

Then make a careful and straight cut off the end of a board. No curves (these tend to deflect the blade). Now check the finished cut with your combination square. If the cut is square, you're good. If it's not, then tweak the base of the tool until the resulting cut is square. Now cut a curve at a comfortable pace and check the work. The edge should be square to the face. If the blade deflects, then slow down your cutting pace.

You do need variable speed at the trigger – the more you press, the faster the blade goes. This is common on all but the cheapest tools.

Jigsaw Use

Like any portable saw (hand or power) you want to have a pencil line that shows you where to cut. Always cut to one side of the line – the waste side. Cut as close as your skills allow. The less wood you leave, the less clean-up work will ensue, but the more disastrous the mistakes will become. I shoot for 1/32" of waste left or less.

The jigsaw is a two-handed tool. One-handed use is for hot dogs. One hand should grasp the tool's body and trigger. Use the thumb on the other hand to press the base against the work. I use both hands to steer the tool. My trigger hand supplies the forward motion and does the heavy steering. My other hand provides the small adjustments that are critical to tracking my line. The thumb also keeps the saw from jumping up and down in the cut. If you keep the saw's plastic guards in place, this is quite safe.

You also need to know about relief cuts. These are the difference between success and disaster at times. Simply put, relief cuts are cuts you make into the waste that allow you to remove the waste one chunk at a time. They're sort of like waypoints for your tool. When your waste comes out in small chunks, it's less likely to droop and split and splinter, which can ruin your work. It also allows you to turn curves that are a bit tighter by freeing up space behind the blade, allowing it to turn.

I usually make a couple of relief cuts where my cutline is heading into a turn or coming out of a heavy turn. Also, I'll make a relief cut when I see that the waste

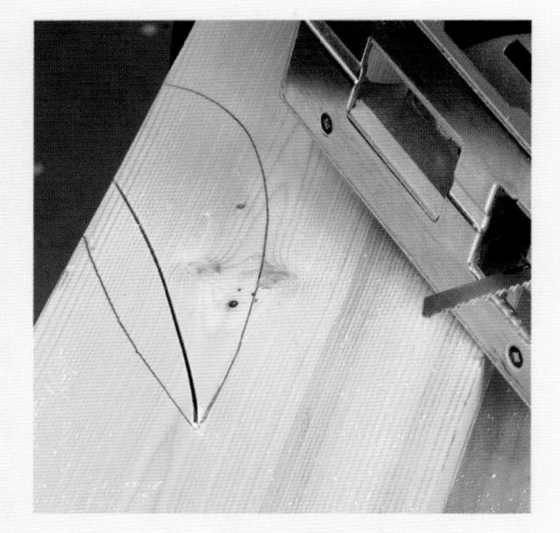

Learning where to make a relief cut takes some practice. If you have a sharp corner, such as this, that's always a good place to put a relief cut. You'll also want a few relief cuts in a long cut to prevent your waste from sagging and possibly breaking off.

is going to be 6" long or so. This really depends on how big your waste piece is going to be and how droopy it will become during the cut.

We need to say a word about blades. Cheap blades will burn or leave a splintery mess in their wake. Buy nice blades and take care of them – wipe them clean with your WD-40 rag at the end of your shop time. After years of trying out different blades, we generally have two kinds of blades in our shop. I like the Bosch T234X Progressor blades, with 11 teeth per inch (*tpi* in shop lingo). Senior Editor Bob Lang likes the Progressor for straight cuts, but prefers the T101BR for curves where the Progessor is too bitey and rough.

MITER SAWS

These saws were once the province of the high-end finish carpenter. Then the rough carpenters started using them (where they're called chop saws) as did the furniture makers. Each profession leans on a different feature of the tool to do their work. Finish carpenters like the combination of portability and accuracy. Carpenters like the speed and power. Furnituremakers like the accuracy and safety compared to a radial-arm saw (sometimes called the "radical-harm saw").

These tools are rarely perfect out of the box. They require tweaking for furniture work, plus they require a different way of working that we'll discuss later. But by and large they are incredible tools once you understand a few things.

Styles of Saws

There are three major saws in the miter saw family:

Straight Miter Saw: This saw makes miters at any angle, usually between 47° left and 47° right at minimum. The cut this saw makes will always be 90° to the face of the work.

Compound Miter Saw: This saw does everything a straight miter saw does, plus the head can tip right (or both right and left) to make compound cuts. Compound cuts are angled in two directions, across the face of the board and across its thickness. This feature is used by trim carpenters for installing crown moulding.

Sliding Compound Miter Saw: This saw does everything the above saws do, but it also runs on a sliding carriage, which allows you to cut wide boards – most of these saws will cut a 12"-wide board; some go as far up as 16". These saws are as expensive as a good entry-level table saw and most of the features are little-used by a furniture maker.

So which saw do you need? Really? Probably just a straight miter saw. These are getting harder to find these days, so you might have to step up to a compound miter saw. And even these are getting cheap. Thanks to overseas manufacturing, I've seen good 10" compound miter saws for about $100 or a little more. What about the blade size? The 12" saws are notably more expensive, though it's nice for the occasional cut where you really need the extra width. However, we honestly think you can get by just fine with a 10" saw.

Important Features

These saws can be loaded with extras, so let's cut through the clutter here. Two things are really important with this tool. First, it has to have a decent carbide-tooth blade that is capable of making clean finish cuts. Look for a blade with at least 40 teeth (and as many as 80). The more teeth you have, the smoother the cut, but having more teeth slows the cut and increases the chance you'll burn the work. And if you fall for a cheap saw that comes with a high-speed steel blade, you'll be upgrading it immediately and probably spending a good deal more money than you have to.

Second, you need a saw that is easy to adjust so the blade is 90° to the fence. Note that I'm not talking about the little handle up front that allows you to swing the head left and right. I'm talking about adjusting the tool so that when the head is locked at 90° it makes a perfect 90° cut. Sometimes you have to adjust the fence behind the blade, sometimes you adjust the points where the head locks down. We prefer this second method of adjusting the saw because it is faster and it doesn't ever result in you bending the fence. I've bent a couple, even while being careful. And when the fence is bent, you'll never get a square cut on both sides of the blade.

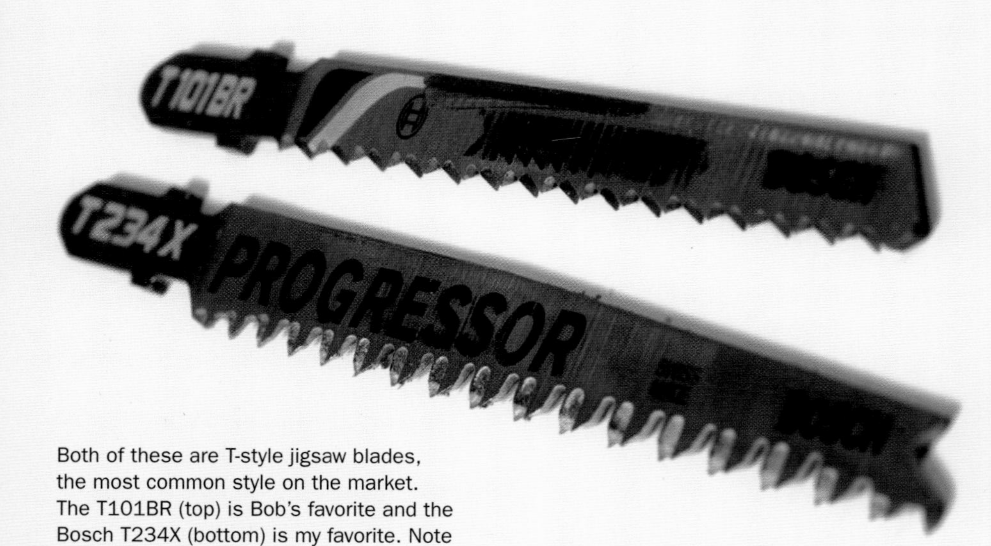

Both of these are T-style jigsaw blades, the most common style on the market. The T101BR (top) is Bob's favorite and the Bosch T234X (bottom) is my favorite. Note that mine is bigger.

Your basic 10" miter saw is accurate enough and durable enough for a lifetime of woodworking. Beware of low-priced saws, even from national brands. One of the ways they lower the price is by equipping the saw with a poor-quality blade. You'll have to replace that blade immediately, and that almost always negates the price savings.

A carbide blade on top of a steel blade. Luckily, the steel blades are becoming more difficult to find, even on the cheaper saws. If you see a steel blade, don't buy it unless you need something to chew up your work in an unacceptable manner.

Follow the manufacturer's directions for squaring up the tool, and then make a sample cut and check it with your combination square. This brings us to another critical aspect of miter saws: How you make the cut. I've found that the number one cause of errors in this tool is not that the fence is off, it's that the work has shifted slightly during the cut, spoiling your accuracy.

The problem is these tools have fences and tables that are make of machined aluminum, which is slippery. So it's quite difficult to hold your work perfectly still during the cut. It's possible, of course, just difficult. Some manufacturers supply a hold-down clamp to secure the work against the table. These can be slow and can get in the way. The best solution I've found is to apply a layer of #120-grit peel-and-stick sandpaper to both sides of the fence. This works wonders.

The other way to spoil your accuracy is by taking too light of a cut and taking it too fast. For example, let's say you want to trim 1⁄32" off the end of a board. You line up the board as best you can and make your cut. It's not a lot of material so you make the cut quickly. Sometimes, not always, the blade can deflect out when you do this. This results in a cut that is not 90° to the face of the board. If you need to make a cut like this, take it a bit slower in order to keep the blade true.

The bottom line with this tool is that it's always best to check your work, especially if you don't have some sort of stop to constrain it from slipping around. So cut each joint and try each joint. You'll be fine.

Other features of miter saws are less important. We haven't become fans of lasers on these saws yet. That may change, however, once they get them

Here's a common operation with a miter saw – trying to remove just a bit to sneak up on a cut line. If you make this cut too fast (especially in hardwoods or thick stock), the blade can deflect. Though it seems like you're making a light cut, slow down and check the cut across the thickness to ensure everything's OK.

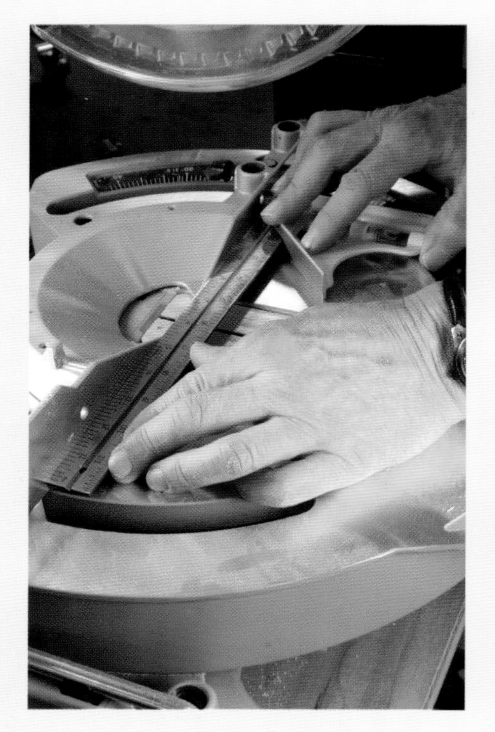

The fences on these saws can be bent during assembly. When you get your saw out of the box, check the fence with your square to ensure it's straight. If it's not, take the saw back and exchange it. A bent fence is almost impossible to fix and will cause a lifetime of headaches.

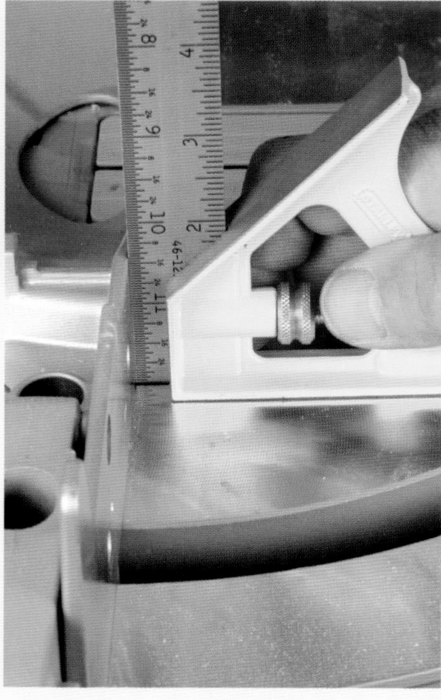

A less-common problem is that the fence isn't square to the table. Check this along several points on the fence. A twisted fence will wreak havoc with your accuracy.

Personally, I don't understand why they make the table and fence so smooth and slippery. Their job is to support and grip the work. Even after using these tools for thirteen years, I still struggle with keeping the work immobilized as I cut it. If it shifts even a tiny bit during the cut, your cut won't be square. Adding a bit of self-stick sandpaper to the fence works wonders.

working just right. The raw amperage of these saws is mostly a non-issue. Almost all of them list their power as 15 amps, which is the maximum for a typical 120-volt household circuit and plug. All of the saws we've tested, even the cheapies, have enough power to cut standard material thicknesses with no complaint. The dust collection on all of them is quite poor – learn to live with it.

A few saws allow you to do stop cuts to make grooves or trenches across your work. You'll probably never use this feature. There are also high fences (best for crown moulding) and gizmos that allow you to micro-adjust your miter settings. These are not deal-breakers (or deal-makers).

CIRCULAR SAW

When we decided on the list of power tools for our tool kit, we selected the jigsaw over the circular saw. But there are many instances where the circular saw would be the best choice; straight-line rips and cutting plywood are the most relevant. So we decided that the circular saw would have to be the first power tool added to that original list.

There is much to consider when selecting a circular saw, the first of which is the saw's size. The size of the saw is described in terms of blade diameter. You'll find saws that are from 4³⁄8" to 10¹⁄4" with a number of entries between.

So, how do you choose? To begin, take a look at the depth of cut that can be made with the saw set at 90° and at 45°. As you begin building projects from this series you'll find that your materials will be mostly ³⁄4" or 1¹⁄2" thick. So, the need to cut these materials should inform your purchase.

A 4³⁄8" circular saw will cut only 1¹⁄4" in thickness set at 90°, and ³⁄4" when angled at 45°. So, it's obvious this saw is not the one for your shop. You'll find that a 6¹⁄2" saw just clears a 1¹⁄2" cut at 90° but because the size is a bit odd, you may have trouble locating blades.

The most popular size of circular saw is the 7¹⁄4". Any store that carries circular saws will have a complete line of 7¹⁄4" saws from which to choose, as well as a

Large knobs can makes adjustments quick and easy when adjusting the depth or angle of cut.

number of different blades designs (we'll discuss those in moment). The depth of cut with the 7$^{1}/_{4}$" saw at both 90° and 45° is more than required. This saw meets or exceeds the requirements of most woodworking so there is no need to look into bigger models that are heavier, higher in cost and unwieldy as well.

Saw Designs

Circular saws are divided into two general categories – worm drives and in-line saws, also known as sidewinders. Worm drives are easily recognizable due to their design. The motor sits behind the blade, which is driven by a worm gear (the gear looks like a curled worm.) These saws provide a good line of sight while cutting and will extend your reach across sheet goods, but they are more expensive than sidewinders. And, because wormdrive saws are much heavier saws – 14 to 16 pounds – they can be awkward to use because they tend to be front heavy.

Sidewinders, so named because the motor sits beside the blade, are the most common configuration. A sidewinder provides a better balance in your hand because the handle is directly above the motor. Bottom line: We recommend a 7$^{1}/_{4}$" in-line saw.

WHAT TO LOOK FOR IN A SAW

So where do you go from here? What about the power? Most saws boast of amps. The 7$^{1}/_{4}$" saws generally have a 13- to 15-amp motor. Amps relate only the amount of electricity that the tools use, not the power sent to the blade. Is that good, or is horsepower better? Horsepower is generally measured when the saw is not in a real-world cutting situation. This too, is not an informative basis for comparison. The better way to select a saw is by price. A good sidewinder for woodworking will set you back around $100 to $150. Sure, there are saws that cost less, but they aren't going to last a lifetime nor be able to withstand the rigors of the woodworking shop. They would be great for the homeowner looking to use a saw occasionally.

Not only can you see the difference between the worm drive saw (left) and the sidewinder (right), it is obvious that the sidewinder will be a lighter, more easily controlled saw.

COMPARISON SHOPPING

In side-by-side comparisons of saws, begin with an inspection of the saw's shoe – the bottom plate of the saw. You can find shoes that are aluminum or magnesium as well as plastic and other material. Our recommendation is to stay away from the plastic shoes and look for a metal base; cast metal would be best. A shoe with ribs will have added reinforcement in case (or when) you drop the saw on the floor – but that added strength adds weight to the tool.

The overall weight of the saw will affect comfort, and that is an issue in choosing your saw. Also, check the handle positioning and the balance of the saw. Making sure that the saw fits your hands and feels comfortable while in use is key in the selection process.

Next you need to look at the adjustments of the saw. The two adjustments are depth of cut and angle. You'll find knobs, levers and wing nuts used to allow these adjustments. Large knobs and smartly placed levers will make adjustments both quick, and accurate. Small, out-of-the-way levers and wing nuts are less handy.

The last issue to consider is how easy it is to change the blade. We've seen saws that require you to insert a nail through a hole in the blade to lock the blade. Or worse yet, to hold the blade as you try to release the arbor nut. These are not the best scenarios. A shaft-lock mechanism is the best option. This feature locks the shaft so it doesn't rotate, allowing easy use of a wrench to remove the arbor nut.

A WORD ABOUT BLADES

A sharp blade is very important when using a circular saw. Dull blades are one of the causes of kickback, which is when the blade catches the wood but instead of cutting the piece, the saw is propelled back toward the operator. This is dangerous.

There are many choices when selecting a blade for your circular saw. First, you should always use a blade that is sized for your saw – if you have a 7¹⁄4" saw, use a 7¹⁄4" blade. Installing a smaller-diameter blade will not allow the saw to develop the rim speed needed for the machine to work at its full potential.

Second, base your blade decision on the type of work the blade will perform. If you're roughcutting lumber, a 24-tooth carbide blade would be right. But using that blade to cut veneer-faced plywood would result in a massive amount of tear-out.

There are blades that have 16, 18, 24, 40 or 60 teeth (and some in between, I'm sure). There are blades for plywood as well as masonry. You have to decide how the saw will be used in order to select the correct blade. Our tool kit would have a 24-tooth carbide blade (carbide tips on the teeth will stay sharp longer) for roughcutting stock and a 40-tooth carbide blade for the finish cuts.

Large knobs can makes adjustments quick and easy when changing the depth or angle of cut. The cut made with a circular saw should not be considered the last step in the milling process. A hand plane should be used to ne-tune most of the edges for better-quality results.

Properly setting the depth of cut will help extend the life of the blade and lessen the possibility of kickback.

USING THE CIRCULAR SAW

There are a few basic guidelines for using a circular saw. Adjust the depth of cut prior to cutting any material. Loosen the knob or lever and raise or lower the shoe until the blade is between ¹⁄8" – ¹⁄4" beyond the lower edge of the material to be cut. Remember to tighten the depth knob before beginning the cut. Setting the depth of cut too deep could lead to binding and kickback.

Because the circular saw cuts with the blade coming up through the material, it is best to cut with the face side, or best side, down. Any tear-out would then be on the back side of the material and away from sight.

Always start the saw with the front of the shoe resting on the workpiece; don't let the blade make contact with the wood until the blade has reached full speed. Move through the cut with the motor/ base resting on the good side of the workpiece, not the waste material side and do not remove the tool from the workpiece before the blade has come to a complete stop.

Another good rule of thumb is to have your workpiece properly supported. This does not mean laying the workpiece across two sawhorses while cutting the

Aligning the blade with the cut line and using a speed square provides a temporary fence for a square or straight cut.

middle of the board. This tool is designed to cut through material causing one piece – the waste – to fall away.

To cut the end off of a board, make sure to have the waste material extended past any supporting surface. As the cut is finished the waste will fall away. In cutting sheet goods you may not want the waste to fall. In this case, support the work from below using several long lengths of scrap

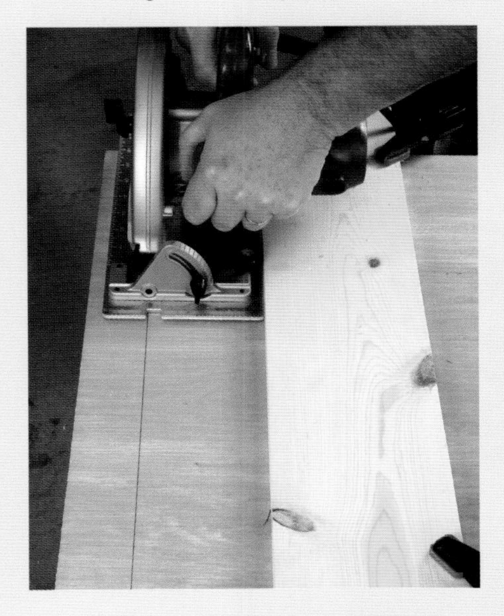

Clamping an auxiliary fence to the workpiece is an excellent way to achieve a straight cut, so long as the fence is also a straightedge. Note the gun shot notch.

so the work is fully supported. Some people cut sheet goods on top of 4' × 8' foam insulation board. Either way, set your cutting depth so you don't cut through the support below your work.

Making the Cuts Freehand

Many of the cuts made with the circular saw will be freehand cuts. This is where the saw is guided by hand and eye, not with guides or jigs. There are two methods for completing this type of cut while staying on your line and making straight cuts. The first is to use your eye to watch the relationship of the blade to the cut line.

With your safety glasses in place, tilt your head and watch the cut. The dynamics of the circular saw will enable to you to make straight cuts more accurately than you can with a jigsaw. The circular saw, because the cutting area of the blade is wider than a jigsaw blade, will help to guide you on a straight path. It is possible, however, to veer from the cut line so keep your attention focused.

The second method of cutting by hand and having the resulting cut straight is to use the gun shot to help guide the tool. The gun shot is a notch in the saw's shoe that aligns with the edge of the blade. Maneuvering the saw while keeping the notch at the line will provide a straight cut – as long as you started the cut at the line to begin with.

Cutting with Fences and Guides

Another much-used method of making straight cuts with the circular saw is to use a fence or other type of guide. As long as the fence is straight, the saw will follow that fence and the result will be a straight cut.

One type of guide is a speed square or an aluminum carpenter's square. To use this setup, position the saw so the blade touches your cut line, then move the speed square tight to the saw's shoe on the opposite side from the blade. At the same time, hold the square tight to the edge of the board to allow the shoe to ride against the square. This technique is best suited for cuts across the grain (called crosscuts) no wider than the square itself.

Making wide crosscuts requires a different fence or guide. The best fence is plywood; the factory edge works great.

But, any scrap piece that has a straightedge will serve. Use the fence just as you would a speed square, but clamp this guide to the workpiece.

This arrangement is one of the best ways to accurately make cuts with the grain (called rip cuts), too. Place the plywood in relation to the cut line as before and repeat the process of running the saw shoe along the cut, ripping a straight line. Be sure to have the work supported correctly.

A Specialized Guide

If you plan to use your saw extensively, we suggest making a fitted guide that is designed to work with your saw for crosscuts or rip cuts.

Why make a fitted guide? Without a fitted guide, you have to do more measuring to position your auxiliary fence on your work. You're always having to add in the width of the saw's shoe when positioning your fence. A fitted guide allows you to position the fence perfectly on the cut line each time.

You'll need a piece of plywood and a straight piece of scrap stock (plywood will work here too) to build this fitted guide. The plywood needs to be about 5" wider than the shoe of the saw and the scrap

The jig has a wide fence to make clamping easy. Because this jig was created using the circular saw, whenever we clamp the jig exactly at the cut line, the result will be straight and on the layout line.

should be about 4" in width, with a factory straight edge.

Attach the scrap to the left-hand side of the plywood keeping the straight edge to the right. Clamp the assembly to a bench or worktable making sure that the single-thickness edge is hanging off of the bench.

Next, adjust the saw for the thickness of the plywood and cut through the plywood as the shoe rides tight against the scrap. This is just like making a rip cut with a fence, but this time the fence is attached. The freshly cut edge is now in line with the saw blade. Each time you make a cut, all you need to do is locate the jig exactly at the cut line and clamp it in place. Each time you run the saw against that scrap, while the saw is resting on the plywood, the cut will be correct to your layout. One thing to remember is that you need to set the depth of cut to the material you are cutting and the thickness of the plywood. This will shorten the thickness of cut of the saw but you get accurate results each and every time. If you need the additional depth, resort to the hand-held cut methods described earlier in "Making the Cuts Freehand." The jig has a wide fence to make clamping easy. Because this jig was created using the circular saw, whenever we clamp the jig exactly at the cut line, the result will be straight and on the layout line.

DRILLS

I'm going to guess that you already have some kind of drill. Maybe it's a corded drill; maybe it's a cordless drill. If I had to own only one drill it would probably be a cordless drill because these tend to have clutches and different speed ranges that make them ideal for driving screws in addition to drilling holes. However, nothing beats the raw and unlimited power of a corded drill. A handful of the corded drills have clutches and speed settings, and I don't know why there aren't more around. Probably because we love cordless drills – they must be the hottest-selling tool on the market.

There are a lot of factors to consider when buying a drill because they are used for so many different things. I'm going to tell you what's important for building furniture. First, you need a drill that is lightweight, balanced and will hold all the bits you need, from the tiniest wire bits up to 3/8"- or sometimes 1/2"-shanked bits. If you are buying a cordless drill, you probably should buy a 9.6-volt or 12-volt model. These drills generally satisfy all the requirements above – except they typically hold bits only up to 3/8" in diameter, which is OK. Heavy drills (such as 18-volt drills) are hard to wield with any finesse. And you are so rarely far away from your charger while you're in the shop that the run-time issue is moot.

You need variable speed. This is found on all but the cheapest tools. Variable

I got by for years and years with a corded drill alone. Once I finally bought a cordless drill, I was glad I'd made the upgrade. Not only do you lose the cord, but you gain some features, such as control over your top speed and a clutch that prevents you from over-torquing your screws.

When you're in the store, close the chuck of the drill that you're considering and take a look at how closely the jaws close. The best chucks will close down to nothing. The lamest ones will allow you to get a toothpick in there. The tight jaws will let you grab the smaller bits that are occasionally important for woodworking.

Maybe the big drill doesn't look so big to you here. Just wait until you have to heft this thing up above your head for the hundredth time. Then you'll want the wimpy 9.6-volt drill. If you work far away from your battery charger (like on an oil derrick) then get the big drill; otherwise, smaller is generally better (and cheaper!).

speed is where the more you pull the trigger, the more rpm you get. You want your drill to ramp up smoothly, though no drill is perfect in this department.

A keyless chuck is a desirable feature. Though the keyless chuck might not hold as tightly as a keyed one, this is almost never an issue. The keyless chucks hold plenty tight enough and are so much faster and easier to use than their keyed cousins. While you're examining the chuck, take a look at the three jaws that grab the bit. Close the chuck on itself and take a look at where the three jaws meet. The best chucks will have a seamless fit. When the jaws come together they will look like one piece of solid metal. Lesser chucks will have a gap at the center. This gap will prevent the chuck from closing on small bits. Most of the time, this is not important, but when you need a tiny hole...

Let's talk a minute about clutch setting and speed ranges. These are important fine-tuning settings that you'll become more sensitive to the more you use your drill. Most drills (with a couple of notable exceptions) have two speed settings, low and high. In general, the low setting is for driving screws and the high setting is for boring holes. That's simple enough. Then you have the clutch of the drill to consider. The clutch has more settings than any reasonable person needs. Perhaps manufacturers see it as a way to get the upper hand on competitors. I just wish I didn't have to do so much fiddling and clicking to get the right clutch setting.

What does the clutch setting do? It's for driving screws. When you reach a certain amount of torque, the clutch disengages the motor from the chuck to stop the spinning action. This disengagement can prevent you from making some critical mistakes, such as snapping or stripping a screw's head. Or driving it too deeply in softwoods – perhaps to the point where the screw won't hold.

How do you use the clutch? Here's how I do it: When I'm driving a bunch of screws into a cabinet back or the like, I'll set the clutch setting really low. When I drive the first screw I'm unlikely to fully seat it. So I click the clutch over a couple of notches and try again. When the screw seats where I want it, I'll drive all the screws for that project.

One last detail on the clutch: I don't much use it in the high-speed range. Most drills have a setting on the clutch designed specifically for drilling bits. So I recommend you set your speed range to high, set your clutch to the drilling setting then go for it.

The list of things you don't need on a drill is quite long. Wrist strap? No. Bubble level? Nope. Work light? Not likely. Laser? Please! Focus on the attributes that are important and you won't go wrong when picking a drill.

Setting the clutch as shown will disengage the clutch, allowing you to drill at full power and speed. This is in the drill's instruction booklet that you threw away.

Keeping your files clean is the key to keeping them working. A good file card (left) will have stiff brush bristles on one face to clean rasps. On the other side will be wire bristles, which are good for cleaning files.

Get a rasp with a half-round profile like the ones shown here. The round profile allows you to sneak into inside curves that the flat face would butcher.

FINISHING TOOLS

After all your parts have been cut, you need to prepare the surfaces for finishing. And that's when you should turn to your files, rasps, sander and block plane.

Rasp and File

Rasps and files are free form shaping tools. They can be used on their own to create shapes or they can clean up the work left by other tools, such as the jigsaw. The rasp is the coarser tool and you use it before you turn to the file.

There was a time in history when a discussion on rasps would be quite lengthy. There used to be hundreds of patterns and sizes available to the woodworker. Now you're going to be lucky if you find more than one kind to choose from at the store.

Files are a little different matter. They are actually a metalworking tool and there are a lot of files available. For woodworking (and the metalworking involved in woodworking) I think you simply need one file; a bastard-cut file will do – either the 8" or 10" length. This file will smooth wood nicely.

Rasps are merely the coarser cousins of files. Finding a good rasp can be a challenge in some stores, but most home centers carry at least one. You'll typically find them labeled as bastard cut, second cut and smooth cut, which is an indicator of their coarseness. Bastard cut is the coarser one; smooth cut is the finer one. Because we're going to do most of the work with a jigsaw before turning to a rasp, I recommend you try to get a smooth cut rasp. Look for one that has one flat face and one face that curves out. Sometimes this is labeled as a half-round profile. This will allow you to shape inside curves.

Avoid the four-in-one rasps, sometimes labeled shoe rasps. These tools have two working ends, one coarse and one fine. They seem like a good idea, but the tools are actually too short for many woodworking applications. Longer rasps are better. You get more control from taking two long strokes rather than 10 short strokes.

In addition to your rasp and file, you'll need what's called a file card to clean them. As you use a rasp or file, the teeth will get clogged with wood fibers. The file card is a brush that cleans the tools so they continue to cut well. Most file cards are like a small hairbrush with two faces. One side has synthetic black bristles; the other has metal bristles. Use the black bristles to clean your rasp; use the metal bristles to clean your file.

One more accessory: a handle. Files and rasps have a pointed tang at one end. The tools are much more comfortable to use if you have a handle on one end. The handles, sold in the same section as the tools, simply screw off and on the tang.

The rules for using files and rasps are the same. Use the tools with two hands: One hand on the handle the other on the end. Like a saw, the tools cut only in one direction – on the push cut. If you drag the tool across the work on your return stroke you will dull the teeth faster and clog the tool.

A good selection of rasps and files. The tool on the right that looks like a cheese grater is a Microplane, a high-tech rasp. They work great, but seem to dull faster in my experience. The rasp to its left is what you'll commonly find at the hardware store. The two files at the far left are both good for woodworking as fine finishing tools.

A typical file handle. Some people swear by them; others never use them. I'm somewhere in between.

The rasp and file are generally two-handed tools. You'll get better control and a more square cut if you adopt the two-handed approach.

After every few strokes, tap the tool against your sawhorse or workbench. This shakes loose the big particles. When the tool starts to cut slowly, clean it with your card file.

When working with a surface fresh from your jigsaw, begin by using the rasp. Always begin your work with light strokes, which will show you where you are cutting. After a couple of light strokes you'll know if you have the tool at the right angle and you can then add some downward pressure.

Once all the marks left by the jigsaw are replaced by marks made by your rasp, you can switch tools. Use the same techniques with your file as you did with your rasp and work the area until all the toolmarks left by the rasp are gone. The file can leave a good surface, but I still usually finish things up with some sandpaper.

After a little practice, you'll find that these tools (even the cheap ones) are extraordinary shaping tools. You can round over an edge easily and quickly clean up tool marks that would take an impossible amount of sanding. They also allow you to easily incorporate sculptural elements in your work that make you look a lot more advanced than you are (and that's what this is all about, right?)

Random-orbit Sander

Good sanding is the modern foundation of a good finish. And a good finish can make an average project look fantastic. Though sanding is a chore, it's something you need to get good at to produce good work as you begin your craft.

We do a lot more sanding these days than our forebears, who used bench planes, scrapers and some hand-sanding to prepare their surfaces for finishing. And truth be told, I do very little sanding in my shop, but that's because I've spent years using hand planes, learning to sharpen and so on. But that takes time, and the real beauty of our modern sanders is that they can produce an extraordinary surface with a far smaller investment in skill.

Oh, there are still some skills involved in using a sander properly and most effectively, but they can be taught in an hour or so and the basic moves are easy to pick up without a lot of instruction. The downsides to sanding with a machine are that it's mind-numbing work and it generates a lot of unhealthy dust.

So if you want to start building today, you are going to need a sander. Don't buy a belt sander – that's for hogging material off. Don't buy a pad sander. These vibrating tools use sheets of sandpaper and aren't very aggressive. Buy a random-orbit sander. These high-tech tools are a marvel. Though they have a disk that spins rapidly, it's also wiggling eccentrically. The result is that the tools strike a nice balance between aggressively removing stock and leaving a fine finished surface.

There are three body styles available: the small palm-grip tools, the big right-angle tools (that look like an angle grinder) and an intermediate tool that's between the two. I have used them all and recommend you get a palm-grip tool for furniture work. It's inexpensive, the 5"-diameter sandpaper is available everywhere and the tool is lightweight enough to use one-handed and get you in tight spots. The bigger tools are better for sanding big tabletops and the like.

Random-orbit sanders are excellent fine-finishing tools for the money and they don't require a lot of skill to learn.

Generally, the variable-speed feature is unnecessary on a random-orbit sander. The only time I've slowed down the tool is when I was dealing with some really thin veneer. That's it.

After some experience with these sanders, you'll want to hook it up to a shop vacuum. The dust this tool makes is the worst. It's unhealthy and annoying. Adding a vacuum and hose to your sander will make your sanding faster (because the dust won't interfere) and (almost) pleasant.

So what should you look for when buying a random-orbit sander? Here's the funny thing, I have yet to find one I really dislike. They all work pretty well. Some vibrate a little more, some are a little slower, but they all pretty much do the job. These tools don't have a lot of bells and whistles available, so I think you can buy a basic tool and be just fine. Some of them are variable speed – I have yet to find a moment where I thought to myself: "Boy, I sure wish I could slow down the sanding process so I could really enjoy it." I'm sure there are some delicate jobs that benefit from this feature, but I think you'll be hard-pressed to say it's essential.

These tools don't have lasers, work-lights or wrist-straps (yet), so that's not a consideration. But one thing you should pay close attention to is the dust collection. Dust collection on almost all of these machines is a spotty business, and sanding kicks up a lot of the dangerous dust – the sub-micron stuff that gets lodged in your lungs. If you own a shop vacuum, get the upgraded filters for the vacuum and buy the hoses that attach it to the sander. If you can't afford a shop vacuum, then you need a face mask that filters out this nasty dust. And not just a paper mask – I'm talking about a mask that's NIOSH approved. These are available at home centers and are the essential sanding equipment.

The other consideration is the sandpaper. Sandpaper can be expensive, but there's nothing more expensive than cheap sandpaper. The quality stuff (Norton 3X and Klingspor are both good brands) lasts a long time. I think you really need three grits to handle most project building. Get #100- or #120-grit paper for your coarse grit. Buy the most discs of this grit because you will go through a lot of it. Do as much sanding with this grit as you can because it does the job fast. Then get a smaller quantity of #150-grit paper for your medium grit. This intermediate grit goes pretty quickly if you did a good job with the coarse grit. And then get a small quantity of #220-grit paper. Again, if you did a good job in the earlier grits, the #220 work will go quite fast.

People sometimes laugh when they hear there is a proper way to sand. After all, you simply put the tool on the work and move it around until everything is consistently sanded right? There actually is a little more to it than that, and proper use of the tool will ensure you get the job done in short order.

First thing to know: hand pressure. Try not to bear down too hard on the tool while you are working. It's tempting to do this when you're sanding a rough patch, but it's not so good for the tool and there's a risk of you going too far when you get rowdy. Similarly, try to keep the tool flat on the work. It's tempting to sometimes tip the tool so one edge of the pad is contacting the work so you can work a small area of tear-out. This will work with a little skill and if the tear-out is shallow. If it's deep tear-out or you linger too long, you will create a valley in the work that may not be evident until you put a shiny finish on the work.

You'll need the biggest supply of #120-grit sandpaper (left) because it does the most work and needs to be replaced more regularly. You'll need less of the #150 (middle) and even less of the #220.

Move your sander in a regular pattern to ensure a consistent job. I'll start with overlapping strokes along the length of the board. Then I'll do overlapping strokes across the width. Then I repeat.

A raking light, such as the one shown here from a desk lamp, will point out the dings and scratches that your overhead lights will conceal. It helps to turn out your overhead lights as you sand critical areas (such as tabletops).

Always break the edges of your work before finishing. This makes your project nicer to the touch and makes your edges less susceptible to damage.

Second thing: Don't move too fast. Zipping around a board with a sander doesn't do the job. Manufacturers recommend moving the tool about a foot every ten seconds (at least, that's what a couple of engineers told me). I think that's too slow to be practical – try it and I think you'll agree. I go faster – maybe a foot every seven seconds.

Third: Work each surface in a consistent pattern. I like to work a panel left to right, slightly overlapping my passes. Then I come back and work the panel front to back in this way. This ensures I don't miss any spots.

Again, you'll do most of the work with the coarse grits. But how do you know when to switch to a higher grit? Once the workpiece looks consistently scratched to the naked eye, I'll take a desk lamp with a movable head or one of the yellow job-site lights and position it so there's a low, raking light across the work and give it a quick look. The raking light will point out any dings or divots or tear-out you missed as areas in shadow. If the board looks good under raking light, then switch grits.

The higher grits go faster. Much faster. Usually, I spend half the time (or less) with the #150-grit paper. And the #220 is used even less than that. After everything is sanded with the random-orbit sander, you might need to do a little hand-sanding with #220 paper in a few areas, sand the boards' edges and then break (slightly round over) the corners and sharp edges of all the touchable pieces. Sharp edges are fragile and don't feel good to the hand.

Breaking the edges is quick and greatly improves the tactile quality of your work. Use #150-grit paper in your hand and take down the corners slightly. A couple of strokes is usually enough.

You should be aware that you will have better results if you cut with the grain. Think of each board like a furry animal – the grain lines are the fur. If your tool is pressing down the fur as you cut, it's like petting an animal correctly. If you rub (or cut) the wrong way then the animal will get mad and the work will tear out.

Block Plane

Buying and sharpening a block plane is probably the most involved task we're going to ask of you as you get started in the craft. The barrier here is sharpening the blade – lots of woodworkers get tied up in knots about this simple and very important skill. Here's the promise: Once you learn to sharpen a single woodworking tool, the same principles will allow you to sharpen a lot of other things: chisels, carving gouges, all manner of plane blades, turning tools, marking knives and so on.

Sharpening is one of those "minute to learn; lifetime to master" things. The principle is so simple: A sharp edge is the intersection of (sorry for the geometry) two planes. The smaller the point of the intersection, the sharper the edge is. The act of sharpening is simply the abrading of those two planes until they meet at the smallest point possible. That's it.

Like sanding, you start sharpening with a coarse grit and move up in grits. You can use almost any medium to sharpen. Sandpaper works well as you're learning. You'll also find diamond stones and oilstones at the home center. Pick a system that fits your budget. If there's an oilstone that has coarse grit on one side and fine grit on the other, that's what I'd get. Sometimes it's called an India stone. Buy a little 3-in-1 oil and you're in business.

The Basic Strokes

There are lots of good books and web sites that can help you with sharpening. I'm going to tell you here how to get a good working edge that will get you started cutting pine and other work-a-day woods. My personal sharpening regimen is different, but everyone's is. The following requires the absolute fewest tools.

Disassemble the block plane and clean off the cutter. Notice that one end is wedge-shaped. This is called the bevel of the cutter. The flat part of the cutter that intersects the bevel is called the back of the blade. The back and the bevel are the two planes of your cutting edge and are what is to be abraded.

Begin with the back. There's a lot of metal here. Abrading all that metal flat would be a massive task. Remember that only the very end of the back is what does

Block planes are commonly available. Paying a little more will add some nice features – a blade adjuster, a mouth that you can close up for high-tolerance work and the blade pitched at a lower angle. That said, even the cheap ones work well on softwoods when sharpened.

the cutting. That's all you need to worry about. So we're going to cheat so that we work only that area (and get to work much faster). Take a thin, cheap 6" ruler and stick it along one edge of your sharpening stone. Now rub the back of the cutter on the stone with the cutting edge on the stone and the back part of the cutter propped up on the ruler. The ruler holds the back end of the cutter in the air so you work only the area up by the edge.

If you use the ruler in the same way every time you sharpen you'll find that the angle stays the same. This is called the ruler trick and it was developed by British craftsman David Charlesworth. It's a big time-saver. Use the ruler trick on the coarse side of the stone and then on the fine. Look at the cutter, the scratches should be consistent and the metal should be shinier than when you started.

Now turn your attention to the bevel. This is the part that trips people up because they have trouble balancing the

By propping up the back of the blade as you work the back, you'll greatly speed the polishing action of this critical surface. The ruler ensures that every time you do this it will be consistent.

tool on the stone on the narrow bevel. I like to use a little jig to hold the cutter for this part, but if you don't have a jig, it's still easy to pick up the skill. Start at the far end of the stone. Rest the tool's bevel flat on the stone (don't forget the oil). Now raise the tool just a tad so you're working only at the tip. Drag the tool toward you. Lift and repeat the stroke about four or five times.

Now feel the back of the blade with your thumb. There should be a little burr of metal curled over on the back. That's good; that means you really sharpened up at the tip of the tool. Work the bevel some more with your coarse stone and then your fine stone until your scratches look good. At the very end, you want to remove the burr. Put the ruler back on your fine stone and stroke the iron over the stone and ruler – this is called backing off. Wipe down the blade and reassemble the tool.

Setting a block plane is pretty easy. You want to project the iron equally all across the mouth. Turn the tool's adjuster to project the blade until it looks like it's just starting to emerge. You can feel this by passing your fingers lightly over the mouth or by sighting down the sole of the plane head-on. Then use a little scrap of wood to confirm your setting. Rub the block over the mouth. You should feel it drag as the iron removes a tiny shaving. And you should be able to hear it. Try it in several places along the mouth. If the drag feels the same and the sound is the same, then your iron is square in the mouth.

Using a block plane is a one- or two-handed operation – I prefer to use two hands as much as possible. Once you sharpen it up, you'll find endless uses for it. After you rip a board with your jigsaw, the block plane cleans up the sawblade marks, making the edge ready to finish (no sanding necessary). If two parts of a joint aren't in line with one another, the block plane can trim the proud surface flush.

Learning to hone the bevel takes a little practice. Take it slow and check your work frequently. A honing guide is a good $12 investment if you can find one at your home center.

A small block of wood can check the setting of your plane's iron. If the block of wood has the same amount of drag all across the mouth, then your blade is centered in the mouth and is projecting squarely – get to work!

Note the grain on the face of the board. See how it is heading up toward the edge being planed? Think of those grain lines as fur. If the tool is pushing them down as it works, the chances are your cut will be sweet.

Joinery Tools: Biscuit Joiners & Pocket Hole Jigs

Joining flat panels to make a box is the ultimate and basic goal of a lot of woodworking. There are a lot of ways to get there, from nails to fancy locking sliding dovetails. All the methods work, and all are valid when used properly. The problem is that most of the techniques require a number of large machines with special bits or blades. We wanted to keep things simple and strong. So when it comes to case joinery, we think you should choose either a pocket-hole jig or a biscuit joiner.

The pocket-hole jig bores an angled hole (a pocket) in one half of your joint with a special bit included in the kit. The pocket is sized and shaped perfectly for a special screw designed for the jig. You put glue on your pieces, clamp them together and drive in the screw. Most people conceal the pockets by placing them on the underside or backside of their work and some people plug them with specially angled plugs.

The biscuit joiner simply cuts out a recess on the edge of the pieces you are joining. The recess is shaped and sized perfectly for a thin wafer of beech or birch, called a biscuit. Add glue to the recesses, add the biscuit and clamp up your work.

Both of these modern gizmos are accurate, fast and easy to master. They both cost about the same and both produce joints that are strong enough for most woodworking jobs.

Biscuit Joiner

Choosing a biscuit joiner is going to be limited by what's available at your home center – most stores will have one or two brands at most. If you're ambitious, you can find a couple more to choose from at a local Sears.

They aren't significantly different at the low end of the price scale – but the ones that show up for less than $100 are usually things I'd avoid. These have plastic fences or oddball ergonomics or are a brand we have never heard of (all those factors are danger signs). Once the price of the tool hits about $150 or so, it's a contender.

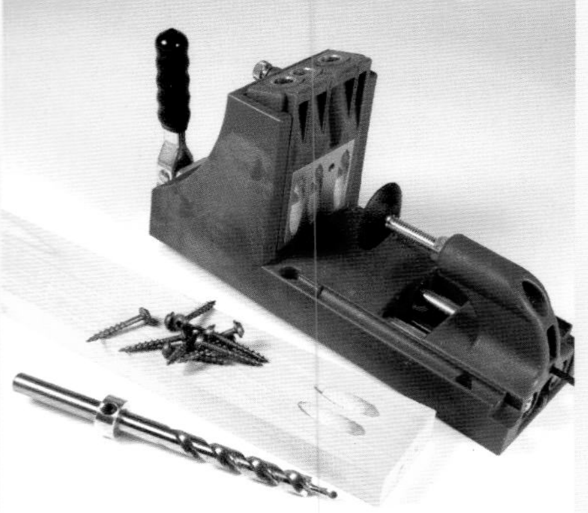

Biscuit joiners (left) cut a football-shaped recess in two parts to be joined. The biscuits fit into that recess and (with a little glue) hold the joint together. A pocket-hole jig (above) allows you to join two pieces of wood without clamping. The only real downside is the fact that you have to conceal the holes made by the stepped drill bit.

Using a biscuit joiner is simple, but you really have to pay attention because it's easy to make stupid mistakes without knowing it. Essentially, the tool is a small plunging circular saw. Press the tool against your work and it cuts one-half of a football-shaped recess. Press the tool against the mating part and it cuts the other half of the joint. Add glue and a biscuit and clamp things up.

It sounds easy, but I've seen a lot of beginners struggle with this tool. The biggest problem is that the tool is not aligned where it should be when you make that plunge cut. It's not really a matter of being a little off on the left or right – the process

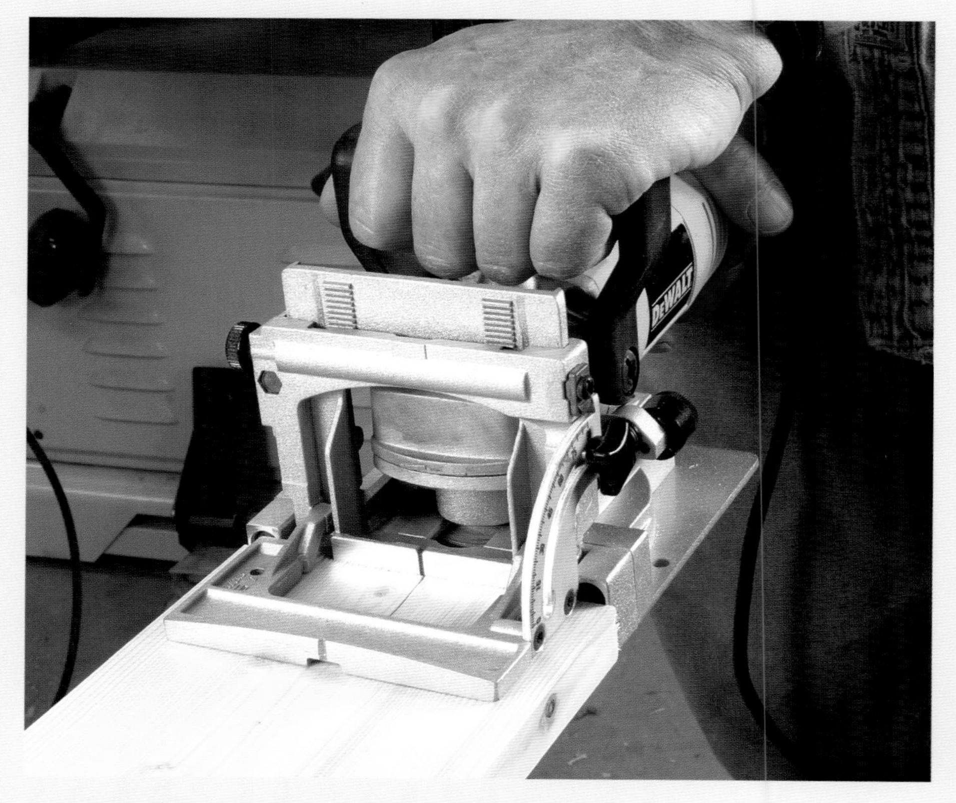

A textbook way of holding a biscuit joiner. Note that Bob's hip is braced against the rear of the tool. He'll shift his body forward during the plunge cut and use his arms to steady the tool.

is forgiving enough to allow you to miss your mark by a surprisingly large margin.

Where most people trip themselves up is in getting the up and down part right. If the fence isn't firmly on the work, or you tip the tool a bit, or it sags a bit under its own weight one of the slots is going to be off. You also can be thrown off by the tool's base. If it rests against anything – and you think you're referencing off the fence instead – you're in for trouble.

I think most problems come from over-confidence. The tool is so easy to learn and seems so effortless that the user starts moving too quickly. Plus, there's the problem of our sensitive fingers. Our fingers can feel a misalignment or ridge of just a couple of thousandths of an inch when pieces are not assembled in perfect alignment. I'm not saying you should be worried about a couple of thousandths – sandpaper can take care of that. But every error (even small ones) is magnified by the fact that it's an easy error for our fingers to detect.

There are a couple of ways to make sure your work is accurate. When you use the fence to position the tool, the trick is to slow down the pace of your work and ensure the fence is positioned flat on your work. Once you have the fence flat on the work, you need to make sure the tool stays positioned correctly as you plunge it into the work. A little misdirected hand pressure here or there can spoil the alignment. Senior Editor Bob Lang is a *connoisseur* of biscuit joiners and keeps one hand on the handle, one hand on the trigger and braces the tool against his body. When he plunges, he shifts his weight forward rather than relying on his arms to do the job.

The other option is to use your hand like a clamp, squeezing the fence and handle to plunge the tool. Personally, I've always put my fingers on the fence to keep it registered on the work. This operation opens up a remote chance for injury, but it does keep the fence in place.

The other way to get around the problem of the fence is to take the fence off and use the base of the tool as the reference surface. This involves working off your work surface, which might not always be convenient or possible. Once you remove the fence, you'll realize that when these tools are used this way they center a slot in 3/4"-thick material. Some engineer or tool designer was really thinking that day!

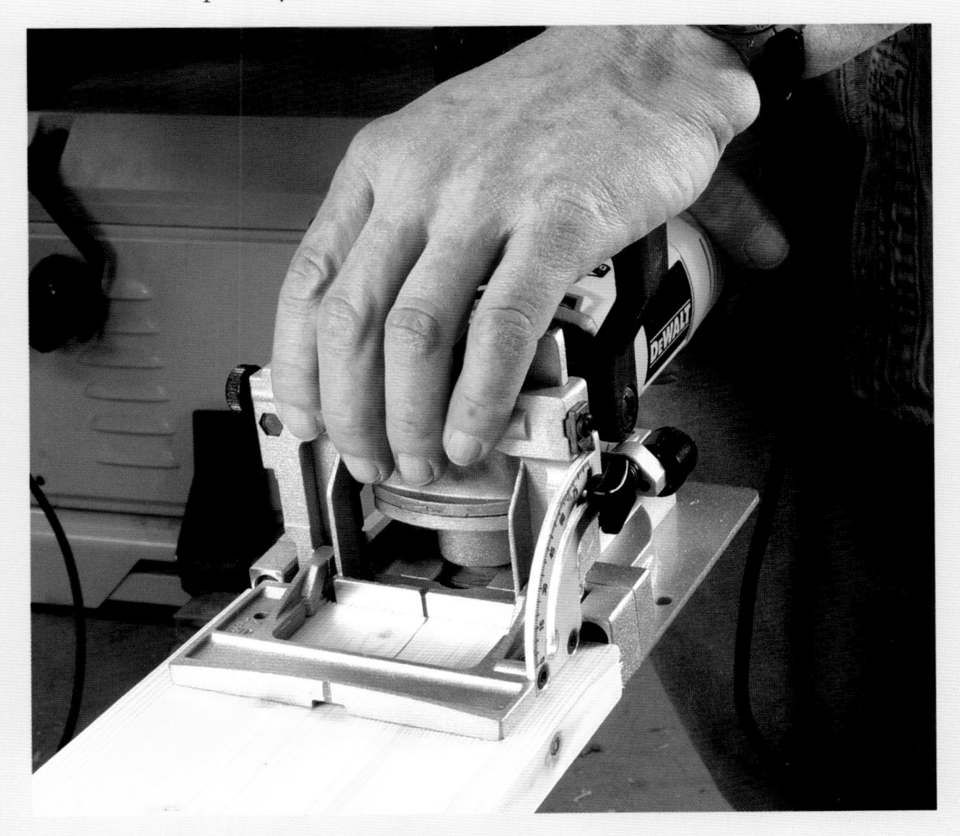

An alternate way to plunge: Squeeze the fence and tool handle together to make the cut.

The other thing you'll find with biscuit joiners is that you have to take care of your biscuits. Keep them in their plastic tube or in a sealed plastic bag. Otherwise they tend to swell and become too thick to fit in their slots. And that really stinks when the glue is out and the assembly is halfway put together.

(By the way, whatever you do, do not listen to the joker who tells you that you can shrink the biscuits by microwaving them. That is – as far as I can tell – a sick joke. We zapped a bunch of them in our lunchroom microwave a few years ago and I officially became persona non grata when the biscuits scorched and filled the lunchroom with a nasty smell. Even when we tried nuking them for less time, nothing happened except the biscuits got warm and a little smelly. Anyway, you've been warned.)

With all these issues, why are we saying it's a good tool? Biscuit joiners have one big advantage over the pocket-hole jigs: they create an invisible joint. There is no hole or screw head visible. The overall work looks tidier inside and out. Usually you can hide your pocket holes inside your projects, but with biscuit joints you can put the joint almost anyplace.

If you never had to turn a corner, woodworking would be much easier. Glue alone will hold two pieces together if both surfaces are along the length of the grain. When one of the surfaces is the end of a piece, however, a glued butt joint will fail under very little force. To reinforce the glue joint, you can do one of two things; add a fastener such as a nail or screw, or cut parts of the wood away to make a joint. Most joints provide both long-grain gluing surfaces and hold the two pieces together mechanically. Dowels and biscuit joints fall somewhere in between. They aren't really joints, but they aren't fasteners either. The advantage to nails and screws is they not only strengthen the joint, they act as clamps to pull and hold the parts together as the glue dries.

The disadvantage to nails or screws is that most of the time you don't want to see any evidence of them in the finished product. If you can drive the fastener from a side that won't be seen in the finished

Some woodworkers prefer to work without the fence when they can. Here we're using the Workmate instead of the fence, to control the tool. If you go this route, make sure your work surface is flat and debris-free.

product, you won't have to worry about concealing the evidence. Pocket-hole screws let you do just that by coming in at an angle from behind the finished surface. We're recommending it as the first joinery system to be adopted in the "I Can Do That" series. It is simple, strong and there are few things that can go disastrously wrong. In addition, it will enable you to put a lot of things together without needing to buy clamps.

Dowels and biscuits are an alternative, but we aren't suggesting either of those for the beginner. In the first place, you would need to invest in several clamps to hold the joints while the glue dries. Every time you move on to a larger project, you will need to get more clamps. The second reason is that pocket screws are simple to lay out and put together, and will keep your work moving along. You can screw a joint together and go on to the next one without having clamps in your way or a long wait for the glue to dry. The third reason is half practical and half philosophical. Dowels and biscuits were developed to make adequate joints in a production setting. Many woodworkers try one or both when starting out, only to leave their doweling jigs and biscuit-joining machines gathering dust as their skills develop.

Because they are a reliable, quick and hidden fastener, the pocket hole screw can often be found in advanced woodworking projects. When your skills have developed to the point where you can cut a nice mortise and tenon or dovetail joint, you will likely still find a use for pocket holes as a utility joint.

The difference between a pocket hole screw and a regular screw is the angle of the hole and screw. The 15° angle lets the head of the screw be accessed from the side of the piece rather than the end. This leaves a large elliptical-shaped hole, but if you plan ahead, you will make these holes where they won't be seen once the joint is assembled. The drill bit used is called a step drill. The large diameter is 3⁄8" to allow access for the screw head and driver, and the end of the bit creates a pilot hole for the screw threads. Because the angle is steep, you need a special jig to control the angle and the depth of the hole.

Pocket Hole Jig

When you go shopping for a pocket-hole jig, your choices will be based mainly on price. What you need to come home with is the right drill bit and screws, a way to guide the bit while you drill the hole, a way to hold the guide to the wood while you drill, and a way to hold the two pieces together while you drive the screws. You will also need a #2 square-drive screwdriver. Most home centers will have a basic kit for around $50. You might also see a guide and drill bit combination for $20. The $20 kit doesn't include any clamps, and doesn't have a fence to align it to the end of the board you'll be drilling. The lack of an alignment fence makes this very frustrating to use, and when you add in the price of the clamps you'll need, you'll be close to the $50 mark.

The $50 kit is a step up, but isn't quite what you need. To use it you must clamp the work and the guide to your bench horizontally. This can be slow and tedious, and it puts your hands in an awkward position when drilling. What we recommend, if it's in your budget, is a system that holds the work piece vertically and that can be fastened to your bench with screws. You probably won't find this at your local home center, but it's easy to find

This setup costs a bit more than the least expensive ones available, and less than the most expensive. It contains everything you need to get started in pocket-hole joinery.

one online or through a catalog. We think the best choice for the beginner or the occasional user is the Kreg K3 standard pack. This includes all the bits and pieces mentioned above, and costs about $80.

Avoid any pocket-hole jigs that use a screw-type clamp to hold the work in place. The one we recommend uses the same locking pliers-style clamp to hold the work to the jig as you drill, and then to hold the two pieces together when you drive the screws. The more expensive kits have a lever-action clamp to hold the work in the jig, and a locking pliers-style clamp to hold the work together as you drive the screws. This is more convenient if you have a lot of parts to drill, or if you are working on panels more than 12" wide. With the Kreg K3, you can upgrade.

When you put the jig together, look for marks on the side of the part that holds the drill bushings that indicate the thickness of the stock you will be using. That should put the hole where you want it, exiting the end of the piece at or very close to the thickness of the stock. Next you need to adjust the clamp that holds the work on the jig. If you're using the locking-pliers clamp, fasten it to the jig, put a piece of wood in place and open the clamp. If it's too tight to clamp, loosen it up farther than you need to, close it and then tighten the screw until it makes contact with the wood. Open it back up, and tighten the screw another turn or two. The wood should be held firmly, but you should also be able to open and close the clamp without too much effort.

The last adjustment to make is to put the stop collar on the drill bit. When you drill the pocket hole, you need to control the depth so that the pointed end of the screw doesn't come out on the finished side of your work. With 3/4"-thick material, a good place to start is with the end of the drill bit about 1/8" above the surface of the jig.

The screw will make its way through that last 1/8"; if you set the bit to go entirely through it can leave a little bump on the bottom that may keep the joint from coming together. Drop the bit in the jig, loosen the set screw on the collar, and slip the collar over the end of the bit. Lift the bit up about 1/8", letting the collar rest on the jig and tighten the set screw. Don't worry about being exact at this point. You will drill some test holes and make a practice joint to confirm your settings.

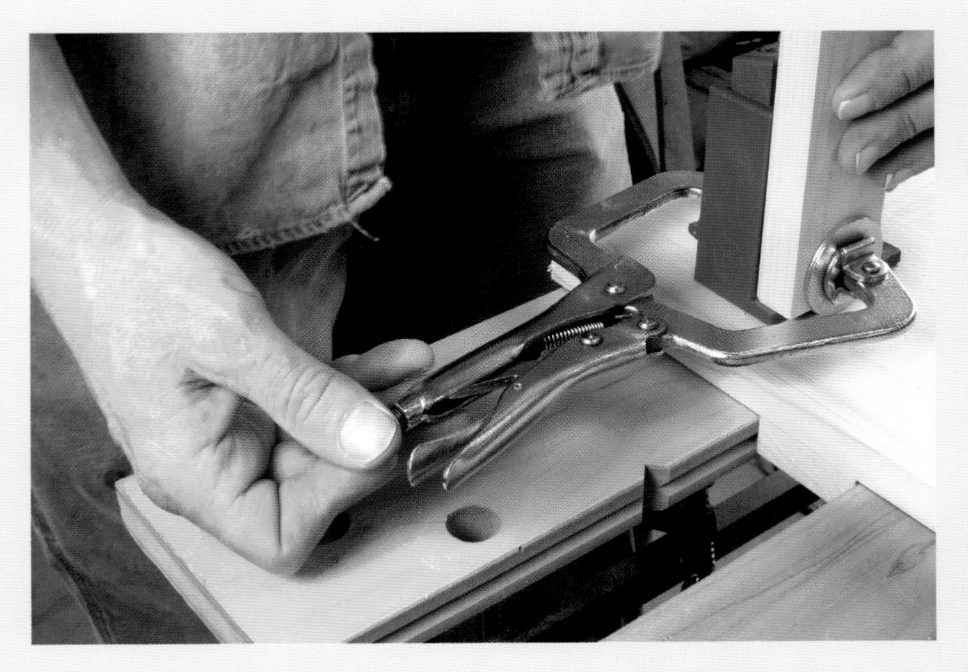

Adjust the clamp to hold the wood firmly in the jig without taking too much effort to set the clamp.

Place a piece of scrap wood in the jig and drill a hole, using the highest speed possible on your drill, checking to see that the stop collar doesn't slip on the drill bit and that the wood doesn't slip from under the clamp.

Remove the wood from the jig, place a screw in the hole, and drive it in. When the bottom of the screw head meets the bottom of the larger hole, you will feel it. Look at the end of the piece. The exit point of the screw should be close to the center of the board's thickness.

Next, you want to make sure that the end of the screw won't come out of the face of the piece you will be attaching. Hold the end of the piece of scrap with the screw in it against the face of the piece. There should be 1/8" or more between the point of the screw and the edge of the

Setting the depth of the stop collar is simple. With one hand, you can push the collar down on the jig and hold the tip of the bit about 1/8" above the jig. Use your other hand to tighten the set screw on the collar.

Use the high speed setting on your drill to make the pocket hole.

The screw should exit the end of the wood near the center of the board's thickness. Don't worry about getting it precisely placed. The next step will let you know if your setup will work.

Hold a piece of scrap against the piece with the screw in it. Check to see that the end of the screw is about 1/8" away from the surface.

wood. If there isn't, you need to adjust the stop collar on the drill bit. You're almost ready to make a joint, but first you need to adjust the locking-pliers assembly clamp.

Open the clamp and then close it on a piece of scrap the same thickness as the material you will be using for your joints. Adjust the clamping pressure in the same way you adjusted the clamp on the jig; open it up farther than you need to, tighten the screw until it makes contact with the wood, then open it up and tighten the screw another turn or two. When you use the locking-pliers clamp to hold two pieces together, keep the larger of the two pads on the finished face. This distributes the pressure along the surfaces you want to have lined up when you're done, and won't mar the work.

The most typical use for pocket screws is in a face-frame joint and the clamp is used to keep the pieces lined up, not to pull them together. If one piece meets the other at the end, hold them in line with your hand as you set the clamp. If they come together at any other point, you need to mark the location with your square, and hold the piece to the line as you clamp. Obviously, the end needs to be smooth and square for the joint to pull together and hold properly.

You need to decide where to locate the holes in the width of the piece, and that will depend on how wide the piece actually is. You want to use at least two holes if possible, as the parts could pivot on just one screw. If the material is 1½" to 2" thick, the middle of the board should be between the two closest-spaced holes on the jig. Once again, you don't need to be concerned about getting the board exactly centered; you only need to be close for the joint to work. If the work piece is wider than 4", use three or more screws. On wide pieces, the spacing between screw holes should be between 2" and 4". Don't waste your time measuring and marking exact locations, it's OK to do it by eye.

When you're ready to put the joint together, apply some glue to the end grain of the piece that the screws go in. As you practice, try varying the amount of glue that you use until you get just a small amount of squeeze out when you drive the screws. Using more glue than necessary will only create a mess to clean up, and can lead to some big problems when finishing. If you're driving the screws with a cordless drill, use the lowest speed available and the long driver bit that comes with the kit.

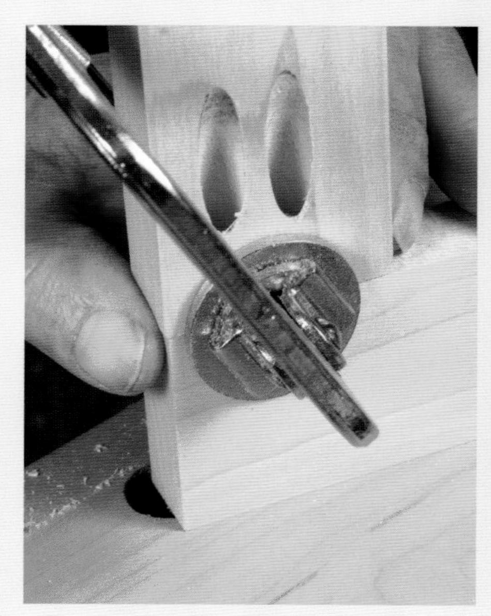

Line up the two pieces and set the clamp to hold them together.

You're not limited to face-frame joints with pocket screws. You can also join pieces on edge, but when you do this, you lose the ability to clamp them together with the locking pliers. Because the screw is being driven at an angle, it tends to push the pieces out of alignment so it helps to clamp them together while you tighten the screw.

One last thing – you really do need to use the pan-head screws that come with the jig. If you try using a screw with a countersunk head, it won't stop when it hits the bottom of the large diameter hole. The clamping action of this joint depends on the pan head stopping so that the threads can bite into the second piece of wood and pull it tight to the first piece.

The long driver bit that comes in the kit keeps the drill chuck away from the wood.

FASTENING TOOLS

Lots of furniture can be built using a hammer and screwdriver. Because these are two tools you'll never outgrow, you should select your first hammer and screwdriver with care.

Hammer and Nail Set

You'd think that there isn't much to be said about buying a hammer. It's just a metal rock on a stick, right? Well yes, but buying the wrong hammer will trip you up. Buy a hammer for making furniture, not some hammer for chipping rocks. We recommend a claw hammer that has a head that weighs 16 oz. and a wooden handle.

The all-metal and composite hammers work, but I find them less forgiving on your elbows and arms. I get sore a lot faster. The wooden hammers are, by and large, cheaper, too. And here's another bonus: You can sand off the junky, gloppy finish on the handle and finish it to your liking. Sanding it nicely up to #220 grit and then adding a coat of wax or linseed oil will result in a hammer that is a joy to pick up. Seriously. Most new woodworkers are loathe to modify or improve the wooden handles of the tools. Hello? That's why they're made of wood – so you can make them suit you.

There are other things to look for, too. The business end of a hammer can be flat or slightly bellied. Go for the hammer with the bellied face – sometimes called a bell face. This results in fewer mis-strikes and allows you to drive the nail in much closer to flush than a flat-faced tool will.

Also, look at the claw. Does it stick straight out, almost straight out or does it curve down back toward the handle? If it doesn't curve much it's called a ripping hammer. These hammers are used for disassembling things – the claw is actually a crowbar. You want the claw to curve down – this gives you more leverage to remove a nail.

Using a hammer is straightforward, but keep these tips in mind. There are two basic grips. One is the power stroke. You grasp the end of the handle to get more bang when driving a nail. If you're after more control, choke up toward the middle

A good wooden-handled hammer and a few nailsets can serve you for a lifetime. Avoid the fiberglass and metal hammers. They are not as forgiving on your joints (as in your shoulder and elbow).

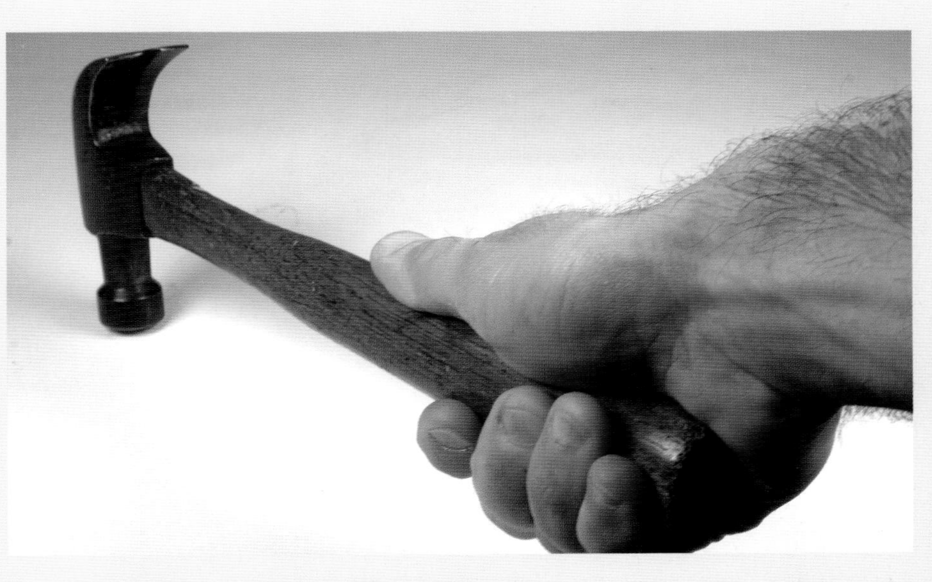

This is the power stroke with a hammer. When you build a deck, or really need to wallop something, grip the tool at the end of the handle. Sticking your thumb out will help steady the tool a bit.

By choking up on the handle you can gain some finesse and reduce the force (sometimes a good thing, really). Note again the position of my thumb.

A decent screwdriver that holds magnetic bits will replace a drawer full of cheap ones and you won't need to worry about wearing it out.

of the handle and extend your thumb. This will reduce the force you transmit into the nail (which can be a good thing) and it will help keep your strikes where you intended them to be.

Also, there's a lot of confusion about how to buy nails. Most places denote the length of a nail using the English pennyweight system. The origin of pennyweight is a mite murky, so let's stick to the facts. Pennyweight is denoted by *d*. So a two-penny nail is 2d. And a 2d nail is 1" long. For every penny you add, the nail gets $\frac{1}{4}$" longer. So a 3d nail is $1\frac{1}{4}$" long. A 4d nail is $1\frac{1}{2}$" long. A 5d nail is $1\frac{3}{4}$" long. And so on.

You select your nail's length based on the thickness and density of the boards you are using. Here's how the old rule works:

1. Determine the thickness of your board in eighths of an inch. For example, a 1"-thick board would be 8/8. A $\frac{3}{4}$"-thick board would be 6/8. And so on.

2. For a wood of medium density (walnut or cherry, for example), pick a nail where the pennyweight matches that thickness – an 8d nail for 1" stock. A 6d nail for $\frac{3}{4}$".

3. For softwoods (white pine), select a nail that's one penny larger. For harder woods (maple), use one penny smaller. This seems complex at first, but it quickly becomes second nature.

Once you drive a nail into your work, you'll almost always want to *set* the nail so the head is slightly below the surface. Then, for nice pieces, you'll putty the hole. The tool to do this is a nail set, which is essentially a pointy steel rod. The shaft is knurled so you can hold onto the tool easily. The tips come in a variety of shapes and sizes. Because nail sets are inexpensive, buy a variety of sizes, mostly ones with small tips, which are suited for woodworking (as opposed to deck building). Get at least one nail set that has a cone-shaped tip. Some finishing nails have a matching depression on their heads and the cone-like tip helps secure the nail set as you strike it.

There are only a couple ofthings to remember about using a nail set: When you hold it, it's best to keep the edge of your hand against your work – don't suspend your hand in space as you grip the set. Grasp the nail set between your thumb and forefinger. Pound away until the nail head is $\frac{1}{16}$" to $\frac{1}{8}$" below the surface of the wood.

Screwdrivers

One of the easiest mistakes to make when buying tools is to snap up a bargain thinking you are getting all the tools you will ever need in one decisive move. This is especially true with screwdrivers. In the tool aisle there will always be a great deal on a complete set of screwdrivers. If you aren't sure what you need, and what the difference is between a good quality tool and a poor one, it's tempting to spend $20 for a set of screwdrivers, especially when a single screwdriver might cost $7 or $8.

You will need the ability to drive and remove several different sizes and types of screws, but you don't want to buy a cheap set and you don't want to spend a small fortune buying a bunch of individual tools. What makes the most sense is to invest in a good-quality handle that will hold different driver bits. Look for one that holds the same short bits that are used for driving screws with a cordless drill. The one in the picture has been in use for more than 10 years, and stores extra bits in the handle. It replaced a drawer full of miscellaneous screwdrivers.

The tip of any screwdriver is the part that takes all the abuse from the twisting forces exerted on it. The screwdrivers that come in sets won't last very long. If you buy an inexpensive set, you will soon find yourself the owner of several screwdrivers with damaged tips (the ones you need to use most often) and a few good ones you likely won't ever need. When you try to use the good ones you have left you will find they are a little smaller than they should be to fit the screw. This in turn will damage these drivers (or the screws) and eventually you will have fifteen or twenty tools that are only useful for prying open paint cans.

If you're using individual bits, damaging one bit or needing a new size or type

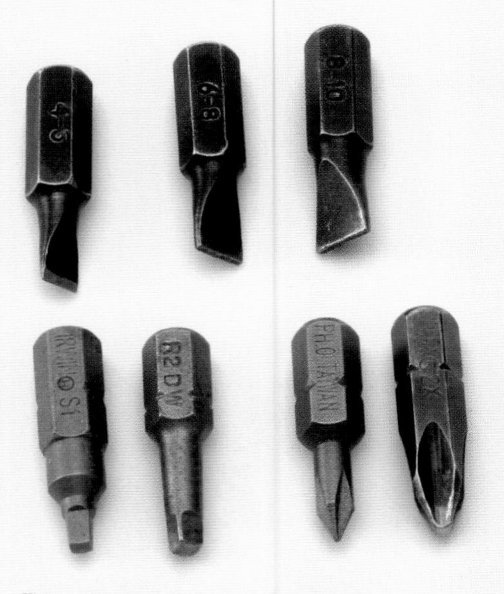

This selection of bits will fill most of your woodworking needs; small, medium and large slotted, #1 and #2 square drive, and #1 and #2 Phillips.

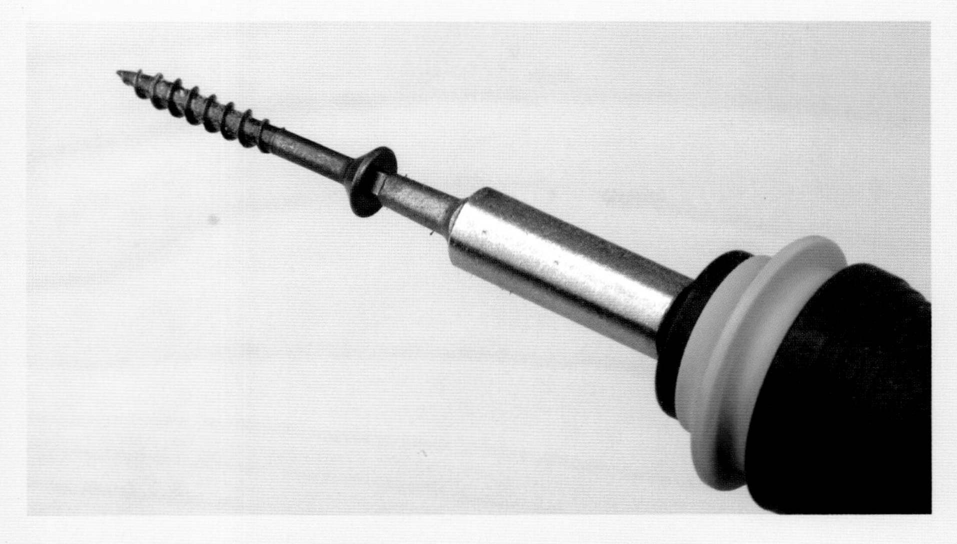
The square drive holds so well that the screw will hang on the end of the bit.

has a quick, inexpensive solution. You should pick up a set of bits of different sizes and types, but once again you should avoid the temptation of buying a cheap set that includes everything you'll ever need in favor of a quality set of the few you will really need.

The one size you will need most often is the #2 Phillips. The crossed recess of this bit is much easier to use than the common slotted screw because the driver will center itself in the screw head and won't slip sideways as you turn it. If you have a choice when buying screws for assembling woodwork, get Phillips, not slotted heads. Drywall screws are more brittle than woodscrews, but work fine in most cases and cost less.

The magnetic bit holder chucks in your cordless drill and uses replaceable insert bits.

The downside to the Phillips head is that the end of the bit will eventually wear out. When a Phillips-head screw is fully tight, the bit slips out of the recess in the screw head. This helps you keep from over tightening or stripping the screw, but it is hard on the driver. Get several extra bits of this size.

The #1 Phillips is smaller, and you won't use it as often as the #2. Usually it is only used for attaching hardware, not in building. There is a wood screw called a trim head screw with a very small head that comes in either a #1 Phillips drive, or a #1 square drive. If you have the choice, go with the square drive. Like its big brother, the #1 Phillips is susceptible to damage and once the bit is torn up, it will start damaging the screws. If you are attaching hardware and can't drive the screws without doing any damage you should make sure your pilot hole is the correct size. If it is and you still have trouble, try lubricating the threads of the screw with some wax. Be especially careful with brass screws. They are softer than the tip of the screwdriver and are easily damaged. Try driving in a steel screw of the same size first to cut the threads, and lubricate the brass screws. There is a large, #3 size of Phillips head, but it isn't likely you will need one unless you are working with large diameter screws. If you have a large screw, and your #2 bit has a sloppy fit in the screw head, you need to head to the store and get a #3 driver bit. Square-drive screws won't slip out of the recess when the screw is tightened, and generally work better than Phillips. A square-drive screw will hang on to the tip of the driver by itself so it's easier to use if you have to reach in a tight spot. You can apply more force to the square drive without it slipping or damaging the screw head. Pocket-hole screws use a #2 square drive, and the trim-head screws mentioned earlier use a #1 square drive. With either of these applications, don't use Phillips-head screws if you have a choice. Square-drive woodworking screws can be hard to find at your local home center, but they are readily available from online and catalog sources. Many woodworkers prefer the square drive for all applications, but you will still need to have other bits on hand. Slotted screws used to be called common screws because the vast majority of screws were made with that type of head. The technology to manufacture other types was developed after the 1930s. The newer types are much easier to use, and less likely to damage either the screw or the screwdriver in use. There's an excellent chance that you will come across them, so having the appropiate bits on hand is a good idea. If you have a cordless drill, you'll probably use it for driving screws as well as drilling holes. A magnetic bit holder will make your life much easier. It's a lot easier to handle and holds better in the drill chuck than the smaller individual bits. In addition, the magnet will hold the screw to the driver, making it much easier to place the screws where you want them. When you drive screws with your drill, adjust the clutch settings so that the clutch engages at the point where the screw is tight. This will keep you from driving screws in too far or stripping the threads. It will also extend the life of your drill.

WORKHOLDING

Your accuracy will be greatly increased if you can immobilize your wood as you work it. And that's why you need some kind of bench and clamps. Here is a bare-bones but workable setup.

Workmate

You need a surface to work on, but it doesn't have to be fancy or even permanent. A couple of sawhorses and a solid door is a primo break-down work surface but I think the case can be made that you can build almost anything on a Workmate.

These wonders of engineering and marketing have dominated home garages since they were introduced in the early 1970s. (If you want to read a fascinating history of the Workmate, pick up a copy of Scott Landis' *The Workbench Book*.) The workmate is going to cost you anywhere from $50 to $100 (or hit the garage sales; they're everywhere). And for your money you're going to get a workstation that can be positioned at two heights: Kinda low, which is great for sawing and kinda high, which is good for everything else. Plus you get a big workholding kinda-sorta vise. It's not going to do the job of a big metal woodworking vise, but with the plastic dogs provided with the Workmate, you'll be able to clamp most things.

One nice thing about a Workmate is that it folds up reasonably flat so you can stow it away or throw it in your trunk. Plus, it's not something you'll ever outgrow. Even if you become a professional cabinetmaker and have $100,000 in tools you'll still find a good use for your Workmate.

There are some off-brands out there. We haven't used them. They might be fine; they might not. You're on your own there.

You won't outgrow your Workmate – I've always had one in my shop. It's a bench, vise and (don't tell) a big stepstool. The new ones are good, but if you can find an older one, you'll have found a friend for life.

Clamps

You need some clamps to hold your work while you cut it or drill it and to hold parts together while the glue sets or you drive a nail or screw. People spend a fortune on clamps, and someday you might also do the same. But to get started, we think you need only about six clamps.

F-style clamps are so named because they look kind of like an *F*. Usually they have a wooden or plastic handle. The typi-

These two F-style clamps are absolutely your best friends when working wood. They hold things in place as you cut and shape them.

The threads on the clamp (bottom) are Acme threads. This is a durable, lifetime clamp. The cheesy threads on the clamp (top) above will strip out eventually.

cal and most useful of all F-style clamps has a bar that is about 12" long with a throat (the distance from the bar to the tip of the clamping pad) of about 3".

How do you pick a good F-style clamp? Good question. I hate – let me repeat that, hate – cheap, cheesy clamps. They usually aren't much less expensive than the good stuff, but they are much less useful and durable. Even if you abandon woodworking, you'll probably keep your F-style clamps to hold stuff for household repairs.

The teeth on the left are on the cheaper clamp. They're coarser and are only on a small portion of the bar. The teeth on the right are finer and there are more of them.

So how do you separate the good clamps from the bad? The first place to look is at the metal screw between the handle and the pad. Look closely. Think of the threads like mountains and valleys. Some screws will have threads with a pronounced flat or plateau at the top of each mountain. Some will have a sharp peak. Likewise, the mating valleys can be either flat or pointy.

The flat-topped threads are commonly called *Acme* threads and are far superior. They are more durable. They don't seem to get gummed up as much. They generally work faster. They are also more expensive, but they're worth it.

The other thing to look for on the clamps is the *teeth* or serrations that are cut into the bar. Cheap clamps will have teeth that are short and spaced far apart. Good clamps will have finely milled teeth that are generally bigger. I know all this stuff sounds minor, but it really makes a difference. Also, some clamps come with plastic pads on each head; some don't. Don't walk out of the store without pads for your clamps, otherwise you'll mar the work.

The F-style clamps will hold your work down as you cut, drill and shape it, though they also can be used for holding pieces together when you're gluing things.

For most assembly tasks, you're also going to want bar clamps. These are remarkably similar to F-style clamps in that they have the same issues with their threads and their teeth. The other factor is the bar itself. Many woodworkers use pipe clamps for assembly chores. Pipe clamps are made from plumber's pipe. You screw the clamp parts onto the threads of the pipe – instant clamp of any length.

Other bar clamps come with a bar made of aluminum or some other metal. Now a lot of people are going to talk to you about how much these bars flex under clamping pressure. Truth is, they do all flex. But here's what's important: If the bars of any clamp are flexing so much that they're distorting your assembly, then there's something wrong with your assembly, not your clamps. A well-cut joint will close with just a little clamp pressure. If you're using your clamps to make up for a poor joint, you'll be sorry later – the wood always wins in the end.

So don't get too worked up about the bar material. Pick a bar clamp that fits your budget and has quality screw threads and teeth on the bar. You'll be fine.

TECHNIQUES

RIPPING

Ripping lumber is a lot of work. In fact, we try to plan projects to do the least amount of it possible. When you do rip – which is the act of sawing with the grain as opposed to across it – here's how to do it. Mark your cutting line all along your board – mark both faces of the board if you can. Use a combination square or play connect the dots. Cut outside of the line with your jigsaw – get as close as you can without crossing it. Secure the board with the sawn edge facing up. Use your block plane to smooth the edge down to your pencil lines. Check your edge with your combination square to make sure you are planing square.

1 Mark your cutting line on both faces of your work – this will help you plane down to the line later.

2 Jigsaw as close to the line as possible without crossing it. Move the saw swiftly yet surely for a smooth cut.

3 Use a block plane to remove the saw marks and create a square edge. Plane down to your cutting line (check both faces of your work).

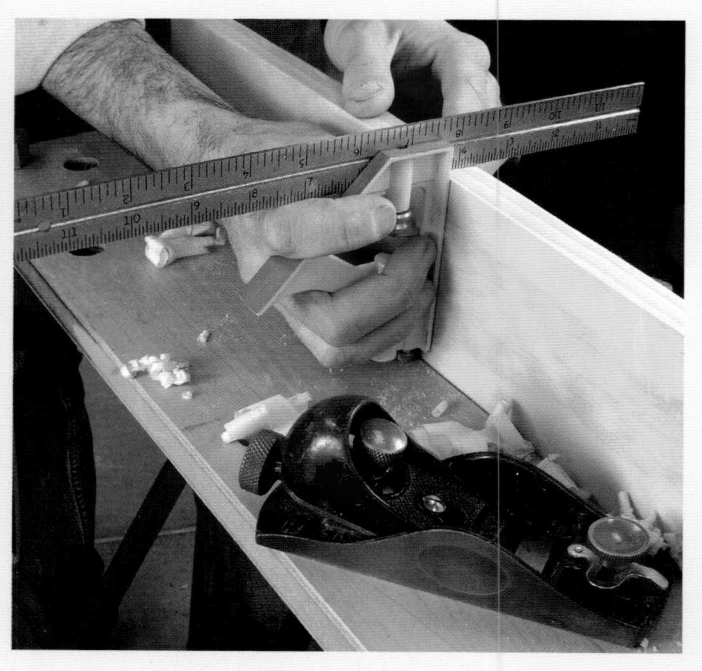

4 Check your work in several places along the edge to ensure it's square. Work on the areas that aren't.

MATERIAL SELECTION

Selecting the lumber for your project is almost as important as choosing the project. Trips to the home improvement store can be overwhelming when you are looking for material the first time. What lumber do you choose?

Resist the temptation to go directly to the vinyl-coated particleboard that some use for bookshelves. That is not what you need. Instead, look up and find the aisle marked "Lumber" – the material that you will need for your project is in that section of the store.

As you approach the lumber you'll notice that the aroma changes to a pungent, wood-like smell. This is where you'll start to notice the many choices available for your project.

And boy do you have choices! In the store that I visited I found that the first area I came to was the sheet-goods section. Sheet goods are plywood, both veneered and construction-grade selections, as well as Medium-density Fiberboard (MDF) and oriented strand board.

Let's look at dimensional lumber – material that is S4S (surfaced four sides). This lumber has had all four sides smoothed and is cut to a specific measurement.

This clearly shows the difference between the #2 pine and the prime of the same species.

DIMENSIONAL LUMBER

Dimensional lumber is an enormous area that we need to continue to refine. All lumber has a grading designation. For our purposes, we're most interested in both #2 and prime grades, which is generally what you'll find at the home-center stores. The #2 grade denotes that these boards have knots that are large in size and possibly loose; the prime grade, on the other hand, is lumber relatively free of knots.

Within dimensional lumber you'll find material such as 2×4, 2×6 and 2×8, etc. Lumber that is 2× is actually 1$^1/_2$" in thickness and the second measurement will be slightly less than the number shown, too. How much less? For numbers

HOW DIMENSIONAL LUMBER MEASURES UP

NOMINAL	ACTUAL	NOMINAL	ACTUAL
1×2	$^3/_4$" × 1$^1/_2$"	2×2	1$^1/_2$" × 1$^1/_2$"
1×3	$^3/_4$" × 2$^1/_2$"	2×3	1$^1/_2$" × 2$^1/_2$"
1×4	$^3/_4$" × 3$^1/_2$"	2×4	1$^1/_2$" × 3$^1/_2$"
1×6	$^3/_4$" × 5$^1/_2$"	2×6	1$^1/_2$" × 5$^1/_2$"
1×8	$^3/_4$" × 7$^1/_4$"	2×8	1$^1/_2$" × 7$^1/_4$"
1×10	$^3/_4$" × 9$^1/_4$"	2×10	1$^1/_2$" × 9$^1/_4$"
1×12	$^3/_4$" × 11$^1/_4$"	2×12	1$^1/_2$" × 11$^1/_4$"

6 and under, the actual size of the piece is a 1/2" less in width, so a 2×4 is actually 1 1/2" × 3 1/2". For the numbers above 6, such as 8, 10 and 12, the actual width will be 3/4" less. It seems confusing but it is a standard within the industry.

Different species that fall into this category are treated lumber, SPF (spruce, pine or fir), hemlock and yellow pine. Depending on your area you might have one or all of these selections. Do you want to use this material for your projects? Sometimes you might.

Treated lumber is meant to be used outside. This is most often seen as deck material. If I were building a table for my deck I would consider using this material, however, I would have some reservations. Lumber intended for this use is treated with a type of chemical that helps preserve the wood when it is exposed to the elements. It is not for interior use. Take proper precautions when working with this stock.

The balance of the selections can be used in furniture, but there is something to consider. This lumber can have a higher level of moisture content (around 19 percent). Moisture is not a friend of woodworking. Once a finished project is brought into the house moisture will dry or evaporate, which causes shrinkage across the width of the board (the length changes only minutely). That could result in your project having splits and cracks.

The use of the straightedge portion of the combination square will help to identify any cupping in the board. Return cupped boards to the stack and select others!

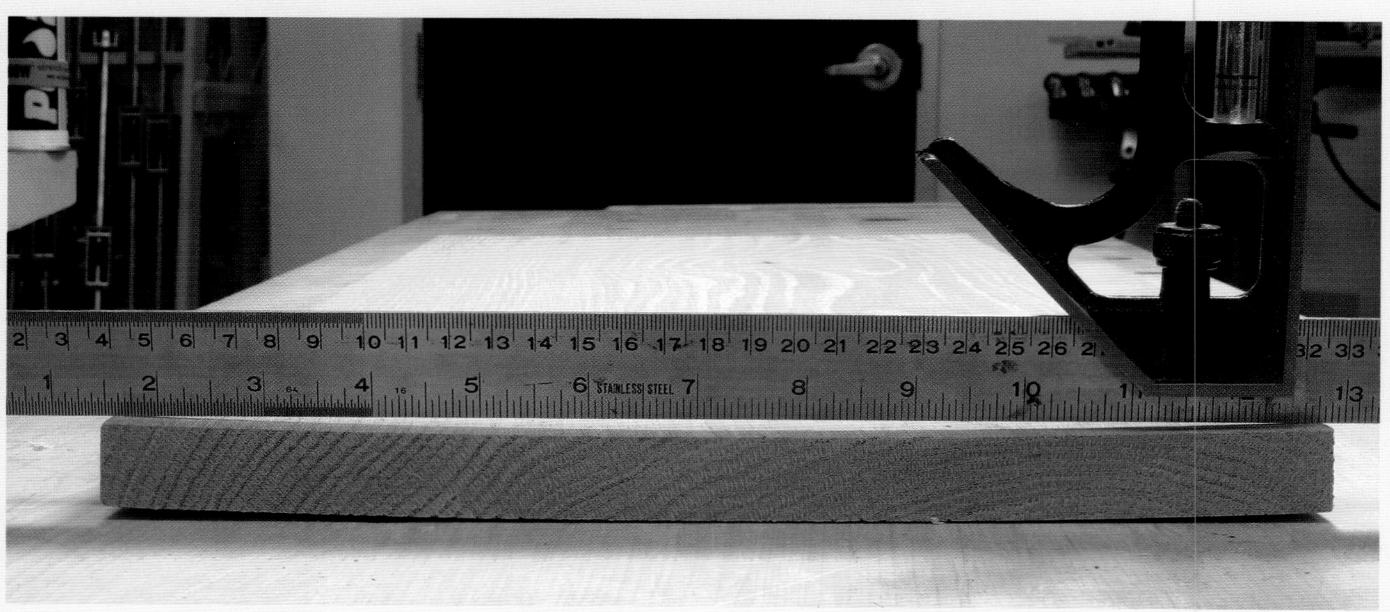

Looking down the edge of any board will help to uncover any defects in the lumber such as twisting, warping or crowning.

If you plan to use this wood in your project, OK. Just let it dry or acclimate to the surroundings before beginning. If you have a moisture meter to check the moisture content, it shouldn't be above 10-12 percent, depending on where you live. No moisture meter? You can wing it by choosing lightweight boards (water makes them heavy) or buying your wood and letting it acclimate in your house for a month.

PRIME(ARY) LUMBER FOR FURNITURE

Lumber used most often for furniture is 1× material (1×4 or 1×6). Here is the good news, the variations between the stated measurement and the actual sizes is the same here as it is on 2× material, except that the 1× is actually 3/4" in thickness. The width variances are identical to the 2× lumber.

Each home store might have different species of this type of lumber for sale. Mostly, you will find pine, poplar and red oak. In my area they also have aspen but in other locales across the United States, they have maple in place of the oak (check your store for species availability).

The biggest differences between this lumber and the thicker stock previously discussed are the moisture content and the grading. The moisture content in this type of lumber should be in the six- to eight-percent range.

Grading this lumber is the same as the thicker stock. In this discussion the lumber from the home stores should be considered prime, however, you will generally find #2 pine in these stores and the knots will be obvious (sometimes you can find #2 pine with clear areas; that allows you to make small cuttings without the problem of knots. And that will save you money).

Hardwoods will be better in quality. Poplar, red oak and other available species should be free of large or loose knots throughout the board. Avoid shrink-wrapped lumber.

Picking & Choosing

Now that we know the type of lumber for which we are searching, we have to determine how we should select from the individual boards.

To begin with, you are paying good money for this lumber, so if you have to pick through every piece in order to get the best board, so be it! Plan to look at a few pieces.

The first test is to look at the grain and overall appearance of the board. If the coloration is off as you view the piece, move on to the next one. If the grain doesn't look appealing, move on.

Next, I suggest that you carry your combination square into the store if possible. This will help you check the board for cupping (bending from side to side) by placing the straightedge against the face of the lumber. Areas where the straight edge of the square is not in contact with the board will allow you to see light between the edge of the square and the flat face of the lumber.

Or, at the ends of the board you can sight along the end grain of the piece to make this determination. If there is a cup in the board put it back and check the next piece. Continue until you get the boards that you want.

Finally, I look at the board from end to end, viewing the piece down the edge, this will expose any warping, twisting or crowning in the board.

Warping is a defect in lumber where the boards will move in one or more directions over the length of the piece, while twisting will cause the piece to not lay flat. A good way to check for this defect is to lay the piece onto the floor at the store. If one of the corners is off of the floor, press down on that corner. If the diagonal, opposing corner raises you have a board with twist. Put this piece back into the rack and move to the next. You can imagine how this type of problem will affect your woodworking.

To discover crowning you also need to look at the edge of the stock from the end. (Crowning is when the edge of the board is bowed, so it isn't straight.) A simple test for this is to place the piece on the floor while holding it on the edge. If the stock rocks from end to end (crown is down) or if it is touching only on both ends and there is space between the piece and the floor in the middle of the board (crown is up), you have a crowned or bowed piece. This affects your work by not allowing you to place the pieces side by side to achieve a larger surface, i.e. gluing a panel together. Choose another board.

Once all the selections are made and the tests are complete, you have chosen a quality piece of lumber for your project. This may sound like a good deal of trouble but I suggest that you make these steadfast rules for selecting lumber. If you bypass them you may find even more trouble while building your projects.

In addition to dimensional lumber, you may also find assembled or glued together panels at your home center. Should you choose these for your furniture? Maybe. The problem with most assembled panels is that they are usually comprised of a number of narrow pieces. This does not present the best look when staining a piece of furniture. But, if paint is your finish of choice for your project – take a look at them. Use the same decision making process and apply the same tests for these panels as you do in selecting dimensional lumber for the projects.

PROJECT 1 BI-FOLD SHUTTERS

BY CHRISTOPHER SCHWARZ

After hobbit Frodo Baggins destroys the One Ring in epic film *The Return of the King*, there's an emotional reunion scene when Frodo wakes up in the city of Minas Tirith and is reunited with his long-lost friends.

While most viewers were transfixed by the hugging hobbits, all I could say was, "Look at those cool shutters on the windows."

After some design work with French curves, we produced this version of the shutters. They are astonishingly quick and easy to build with a minimum number of tools, off-the-rack pine and hinges. The most complex part of this project is in the planning.

Begin by measuring carefully the height and width of your window opening. Measure at the top, bottom, left and right. Now you need to figure out how wide your boards should be to do little or no ripping. All dimensional stock is undersized. You'll probably want to choose a combination of 1 × 4s (which are really 3½" wide), 1 × 6s (5½" wide) and 1 × 8s (7½" wide) to cover your window. Don't forget to allow for the gap created by the hinges. Each row of hinges will add about 3⁄16" to the overall width of your shutters.

Cut your boards to width and length. If you are going to make more than a few of these, I would make a cardboard or wooden pattern of the designs for the leaves and the bloom. Lay out the bloom at the top of the shutter. Measure the remaining height on your shutter and position the leaves in the middle of that height. Make a few practice cuts on scraps first. Then, cut out the leaves and the large part of the bloom with your jigsaw.

The stamens of the bloom are easier than they look. With a nail or awl, prick the center of each hole shown on the illustrations. Drill a 3⁄8"-diameter hole with a brad-point bit at each location. Connect the two holes with pencil lines and jigsaw out the waste. Clean up all your jigsaw cuts with a file, rasp and sandpaper. Sand your shutters.

Join the mating pairs of shutters with your hinges. If your shutters are less than 48" high you can use two hinges. Bigger shutters need three hinges. Now add the hinges that will connect the shutters to the window. To hang the shutters, use commercial wooden shims to position the shutters in the opening and hold them there while you mark the location for the hinges on the window frame. You might have to tweak the edges with a block plane to get everything to fit. A magnetic catch at top and bottom does wonders to hold the shutters closed and in line with one another. Finish them to suit your castle's decor.

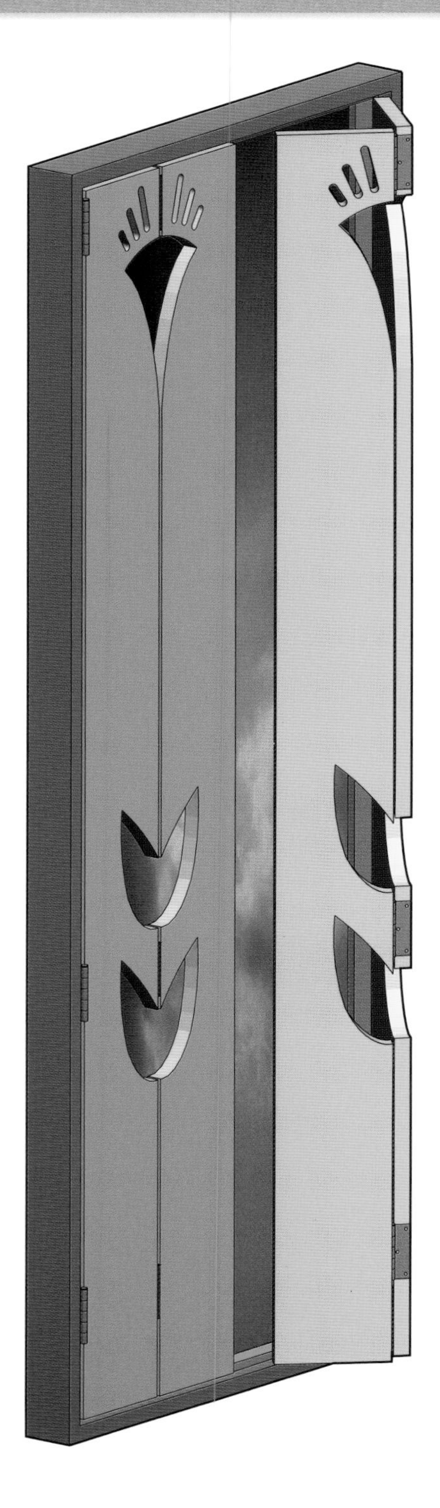

SUPPLIES

Any Home Center/Hardware Store

6 · Stanley utility hinges, 2 ½", zinc finish #819060, $2.59/pair

4 · 1 × 6 × 8' select white pine boards, $13.95 each. Choose No. 2 boards if you're going to paint them or want a more rustic look.

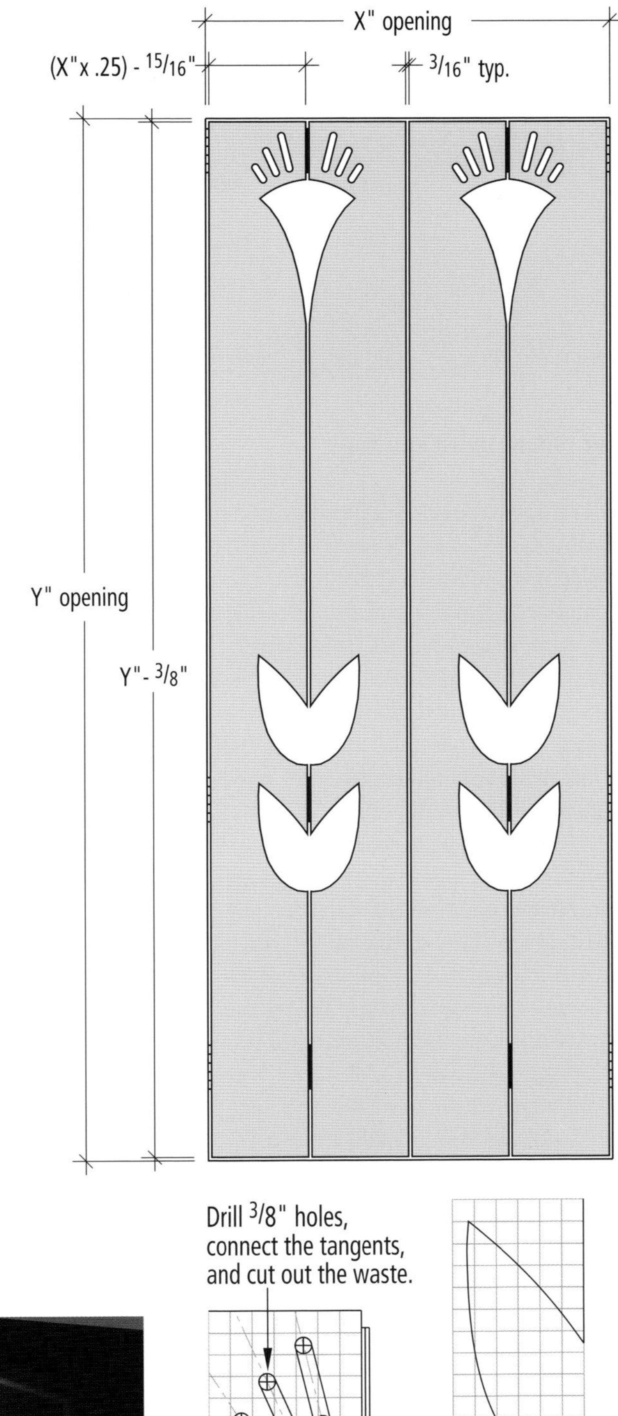
X" opening
(X"x .25) - 15/16"
3/16" typ.
Y" opening
Y"- 3/8"

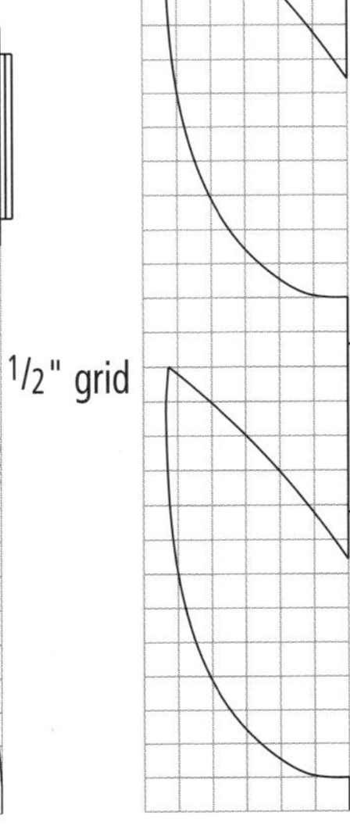
Drill 3/8" holes,
connect the tangents,
and cut out the waste.
1/2" grid

MAGAZINE RACK

PROJECT 2

BY CHRISTOPHER SCHWARZ

Because you're holding this magazine, chances are you could use a magazine rack by your favorite chair to hold your current crop of periodicals and catalogs.

And because you like magazines, I suspect that you also like books, and you might have need for a stand to hold open your favorite reference book – whether that's a dictionary, *Baking Illustrated* or *Tage Frid Teaches Woodworking*.

If you're nodding your head in agreement to either of the above statements, we have one project that can scratch both itches. This simple project has only two parts and they interlock: Slide them together one way and they make a magazine rack; slide them together the other way and they make a bookstand.

And here's the best part: You need only a handful of tools to make this project. Plus, it's a quick job; I built the version shown here in just a couple of hours. It's the perfect "I Can Do That" project.

Gather Your Materials

As with all "I Can Do That" projects, we bought all our materials from the local home center. So with a construction drawing in hand I hit the lumber section. I wasn't happy with the No. 2 pine in the racks. The poplar was an uninspiring purple. But there were a of couple promising red oak 1 × 12s. These were expensive: $40 for a 6' length. But that was enough to make two racks, so I pulled the trigger.

Make a Simple Jig

This project requires you to set the base of your jigsaw at 35° to the blade, sometimes tilted left and sometimes tilted right. To make these changes quickly and reliably, I made a little jig from a scrap. You don't have to make the jig for this project, but it sure makes life easier.

My blade-setting jig was made from a scrap piece of 3/4"-thick plywood that was about 3" wide and 12" long. I cut one end at 90° on my miter saw. Then I set the saw to make a 35° miter and cut off about 3" of the plywood. The piece that fell off is the jig for setting the blade.

By placing the jig on the saw's base you can tilt the base to 35° left or right. And you can use the square edge of the jig to return the saw's blade to 90°.

Make Your Straight Cuts

Use the drawing to lay out all your cuts. With the blade set at 90°, make the cuts that define the two feet on one piece and the single foot on the other piece.

Then make the square-shaped cutouts on each piece. Here's how: Drill a couple of 3/8"-diameter holes near the corners of the square-shaped cutout. Then use your jigsaw to remove the waste and square up the corners.

Make Your Bevel Cuts

Tilt the jigsaw's base to 35° left and make all the cuts you can with the blade tilted this direction. Then tilt the blade the other direction and make the remainder of the cuts on the two pieces. In the end you'll have some waste hanging onto your work that needs to be removed with a coping saw. It's simple work. If you don't have a coping saw, use a chisel and a mallet to pop out the waste.

Clean up all your cuts with a rasp, file and sandpaper. Then fit the two parts together – you might have to adjust a few edges with a rasp to get a good fit. If the part with the single leg is just a little too thick to fit through the slot in the other leg, reduce the thickness of the single leg with your block plane until everything fits. Sand all your parts and add a clear finish (or stain or paint).

In our office, we have far too many magazines for this project to be useful to us. So we're going to use it as a stand for the office dictionary, which settles our debates on word usage. But if we ever need a magazine stand, it's just a flip of the pieces away.

1 This scrap of wood acts as a reliable way to set your jigsaw's base to 35°. I found a protractor difficult to balance on the base and not nearly as accurate.

2 With a coping saw you can rotate the blade in its frame to make a tricky cut like this easy.

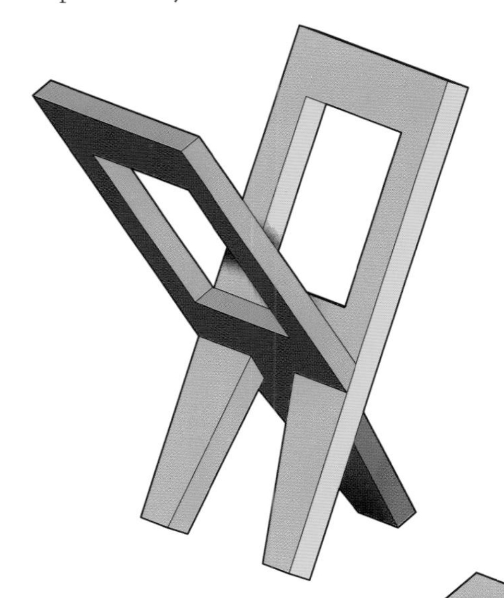

* 35° bevel cut on these edges

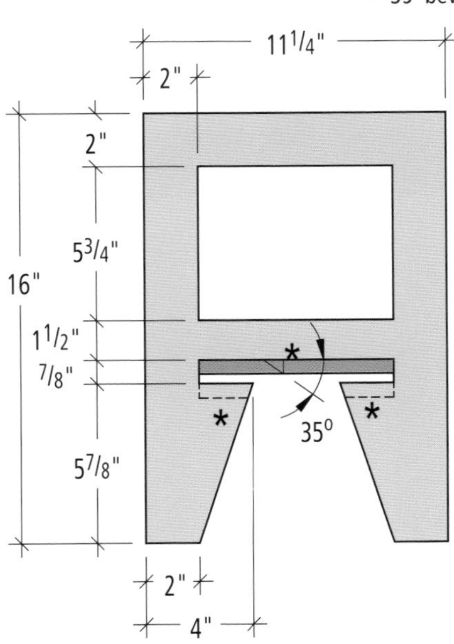

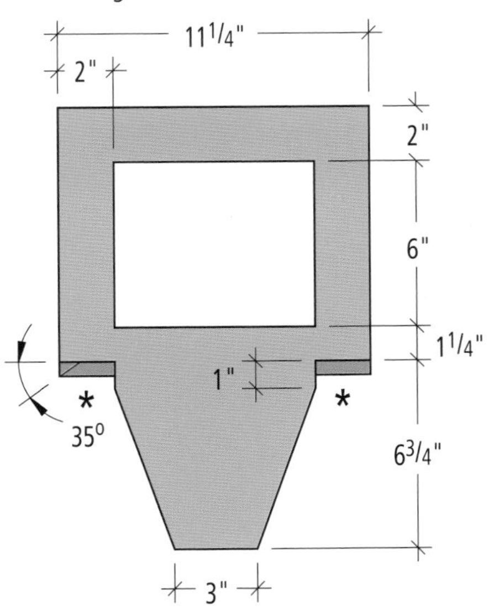

PARTS LIST

NO.	PART	STOCK	THICKNESS X WIDTH X LENGTH INCHES	MILLIMETERS
2	interlocking sides	red oak	$^3/_4 \times 11^1/_4 \times 16$	19 × 286 × 406

BY ROBERT W. LANG

The premise for our new "I Can Do That" column is that you don't need a lot of tools or experience to make a good-looking, functional project. For these shelves, we decided to put our theory to the test, and dragged the non-woodworkers on our staff out to the shop. In an afternoon, they were nearly ready to assemble a set of egg crate shelves.

The name for these shelves comes from the simple joint that holds them together, also called a half-lap joint. Each half of the joint is a notch that fits over the other piece. When put together, the two notches interlock, making a very strong and stable structure. The good news for the beginner is that these don't have to fit perfectly to work effectively.

While this isn't the fanciest joint in woodworking, it's strong and forgiving, and a good opportunity to learn about laying out and cutting joints. But before we get to cutting the joints, let's look at the design.

The material is 1 × 6 poplar, which actually measures $\frac{3}{4}$" × $5\frac{1}{4}$". All of the parts for a set of shelves as shown can be cut from two 8'-long pieces. This width of material is good for holding CDs, DVDs, paperback books or small objets d'art. Some of our staff members chose to use wider 1 × 8 material to better hold larger books. In either case, using the width as it comes from the home center or lumberyard greatly simplifies the work.

The shelves can be adapted in size for different purposes. A simple version with just two uprights and two shelves works well in the bathroom or as a desk accessory, while a larger version can be hung on a wall. You can tailor the depth, height and width to suit your needs or sense of style.

Leave at least 2" of board length past any joints; there is a chance that the wood beyond the joint can split when put

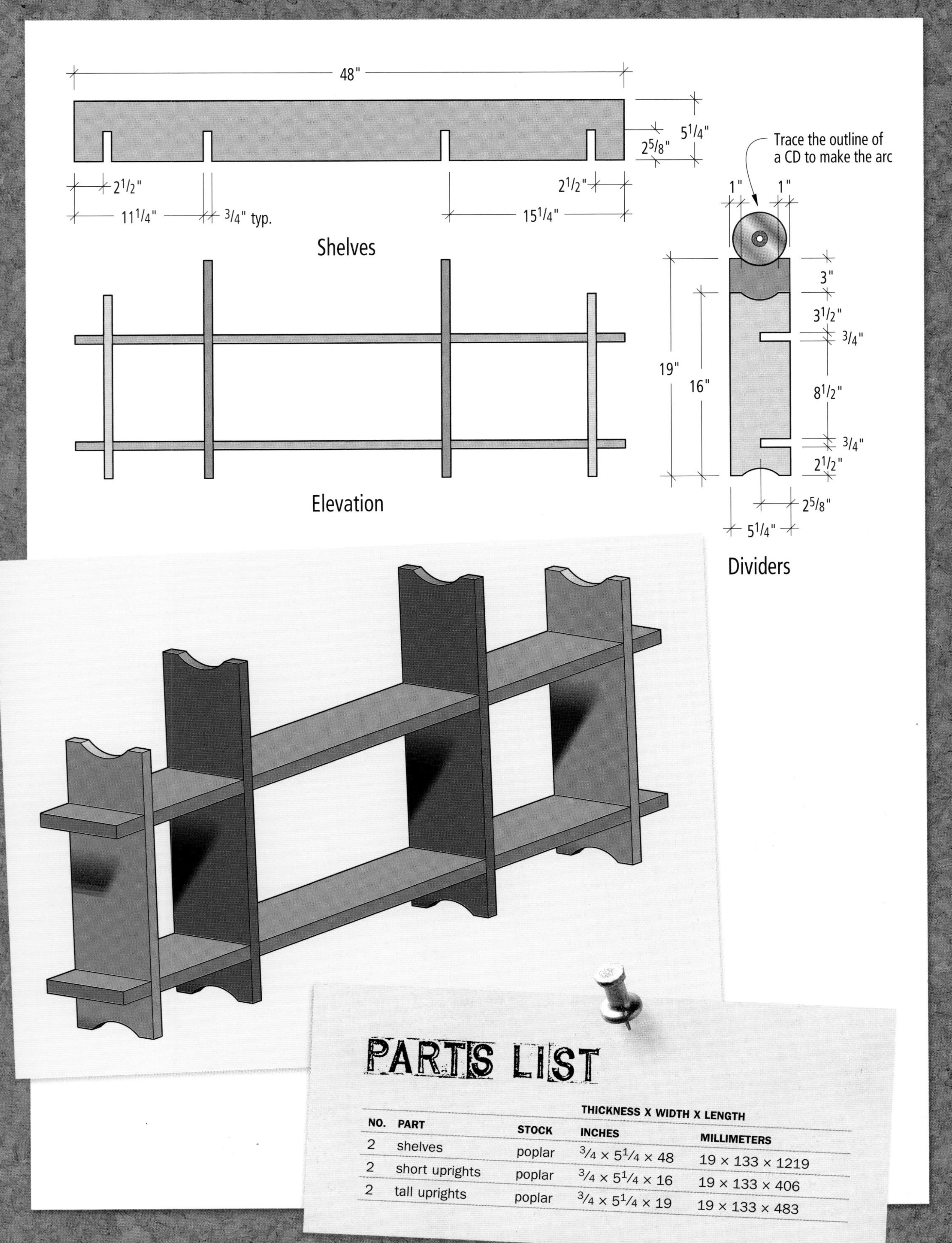

PARTS LIST

NO.	PART	STOCK	THICKNESS X WIDTH X LENGTH INCHES	MILLIMETERS
2	shelves	poplar	3/4 × 5 1/4 × 48	19 × 133 × 1219
2	short uprights	poplar	3/4 × 5 1/4 × 16	19 × 133 × 406
2	tall uprights	poplar	3/4 × 5 1/4 × 19	19 × 133 × 483

Measuring isn't always the best way to work accurately. Holding a block of scrap against the blade of the square guarantees that the line drawn will represent the thickness of the piece that will fit in the notch. It's much more important that the slot and the shelf be identical in size than it is to know the exact thickness of the shelf. Every time you measure and mark something you introduce the opportunity to make a mistake. I consider measuring to be a last resort, and avoid it when I can.

together. To make assembly easier and prevent sagging, keep the space between joints less than 24".

The two key elements for success in this project are getting the notches in the proper place, and making them the correct size. We have a trick to make each of those easier, and there are enough joints to give you plenty of practice. Our beginners struggled with the first few cuts, but by the end of the day they were getting good results quickly.

Layout

Long before the term ergonomics was invented, the combination square was designed to neatly fit the hand. In the egg crate shelf project, the square is used in several different ways, many of them with the left hand holding the square. Once you get used to using it and the way it works, you can use it as an all-purpose layout and marking guide. Find a comfortable way to hold it firmly against the edge of your material.

We want the joints to be in the same place on all the parts, even if our measurements are off a little. By clamping all of the uprights together, we can measure and mark the locations of joints only once, then use the square to transfer the marks to all the pieces by drawing a line across the edges of the boards. This saves time, and it also guarantees that the locations marked are in the same place on each piece.

Next we want to be sure that the slot we cut is the same size as the thickness of our wood. It isn't safe to assume that the 3/4" material really is that size, so use a piece of scrap to get the size right, even if the material is too thick or too thin. Draw a line to represent one edge of the notch, and slide the blade of the square over to barely cover the line.

Holding the square firmly in place, the scrap is placed against it, and a pencil line is drawn against the scrap's edge as seen in the photo (top). After drawing the line, you can remove the square and look down on the scrap and the two lines. If you can see both lines against the edge of the scrap, your layout is accurate.

If we're confident that the shelf will fit between the lines, then we can preserve the lines until the final fitting, cutting inside of them, and trimming down to them. The lines will let us know if our cuts are straight, and show how much more material we have left to remove.

Clamp the board to your workbench, hold the square with one hand and jigsaw in the other and cut on the inside of the lines.

Move the square and make the second cut on the inside of the line.

The ends of the notches need to be marked, and we'll use the end of the blade of the square as our guide after we adjust it to be centered in the width of the board. Measuring will get us close, but not exactly there. Make your best guess as to the center measurement, and make a mark with your pencil.

Adjust the blade of the square to meet that mark, and draw a short line against the end of the blade. Now, flip the square over so that it's against the opposite edge of the board, and make a second mark. If these two lines coincide, you got lucky and hit the center on your first try. Chances are there's a gap between the two. Adjust the blade again, trying to place the end of it between the two marks. When you have it set, make a mark from each edge as you did before. You should be able to get the lines to meet in a couple of attempts.

We can also use the square to guide the jigsaw (opposite page, bottom photos) to make straighter cuts than we could make if we were trying to saw freehand. Clamp the board down, and with the square in one hand, and the jigsaw in the other, line up the saw so that the blade is just inside one of the lines.

Cutting Joints

Back the saw away from the line while holding the square firmly against the edge of the board. Turn on the saw and push it in against the blade of the square to make the cut. Hold the base of the saw flat, and release the trigger when you get to the line at the end of the notch.

Making the square cut at the end of the notch seems impossible. There isn't a way to start the cut on the line, so you need to create some space for the blade. Run the sawblade down one of the previously cut lines, and aim for a corner. After the waste piece falls away, you have room to turn the saw as you head to the other corner. It may take a few times going back and forth, but eventually you can cut to the line. If you go too far, or end up with some ugliness, don't worry. This end of the joint will be covered up when you put the pieces together.

Fitting Joints

We used a rasp to clean up the saw cuts, removing material back to the pencil lines. Holding it in both hands as shown (lower left) helps to keep it square to the face of the board. When you get close, take a piece of scrap and see if you can fit it in the notch (lower right). If you can get it

With the waste piece cut away, it's a simple matter to come back and nibble away the end of the cut to leave a square end to the notch. After a little practice with the jigsaw, this technique will be second nature to you.

Using both hands helps to keep the rasp in a vertical position. Remove material evenly with long strokes of the rasp until you are down to the layout lines. Working to the lines will help you to keep the edges of the notches straight.

Test fit each joint as you go by fitting a piece of scrap wood. Take note of where the joints are too loose or too tight and correct your technique when you cut the next joint. Don't worry if the first joints have some gaps. The project will still come together if you're not perfect. The idea is to practice and get better with each attempt.

One simple joint is all it takes to build these shelves. The decorative cut is laid out by tracing the edge of a CD.

in with the pressure of your hand, you're ready to move on to the next joint.

If the scrap won't fit with hand pressure, take a close look at the joint and layout lines. Take a few more strokes with the rasp and try again. By checking the fit of each notch as you cut it, you will increase the chances of the entire project fitting together, and you will get instant feedback on your sawing technique.

The arched cutouts at the top and bottom of the upright pieces were marked, then cut with the jigsaw. Make a pencil mark 1" in from each edge, line a CD up to the pencil marks, and draw the curved line. (If you're building wider shelves, choose an item with a larger radius to guide your line, such as a gallon paint can.) Cut just shy of the line, and use a rasp and sandpaper to smooth the curve.

When all the notches are cut, sand the wide surfaces of the parts, and make a test fit of the entire assembly. The pieces should slide together by pushing them by hand. If they stick somewhere, take a close look at the location and make a pencil mark along the intersection. Take it apart, and with the rasp trim down to your pencil marks.

When you're satisfied that you have a good fit, pull the joints apart about halfway, spread some glue carefully on the inside surfaces of the joints, then put the joints back together.

The shelves shown in the photo were stained with gel stain then sprayed with lacquer from an aerosol can. Some of our staff opted to paint their shelves. Like the layout, the finish is up to you.

WHALE TAIL SHELVES PROJECT 4

BY MEGAN FITZPATRICK

These classic shelves are easy to build thanks to the pocket-hole joints that attach the shelves to the sides. While pocket holes aren't a traditional joint, they allow you to build pieces that might otherwise be too complex. (If so inclined you could even build a kitchen using pocket-hole joinery, but the screws would add up in cost).

To build these shelves, based on a design from Contributing Editor Troy Sexton, buy two 8'-long 1 × 6s (which actually measure approximately 3/4" × 5 1/2"). Sight down the boards to check for cupping or twisting. And while you're at the home center, pick up a couple of hangers so you don't have to make a second trip (at least it got me out of the office).

Before you start cutting, make a pattern for the sides. Cut a piece of cardboard to 5" × 26" (just a wee bit bigger than the shelf side) and draw a 1" grid on it. Using the grid as your guide, copy the curve from the pattern (page 52) onto your full-size grid. Use a utility knife to cut out the pattern, employing a fluid hand motion. It's better to make a few light cuts than to try to cut through the several paper layers in the cardboard all at once.

Now use your miter saw to crosscut three 27" pieces of wood for the shelf sides (it's always good to have a spare).

Put double-sided tape on two of the boards (this will help keep them from slipping) then clamp them together and trace the pattern on top. Use your jigsaw to make a few relief cuts at the top and bottom of the curves, as shown (page 53), then cut along the edge of the pattern. When finished, clean up the edges with your rasp, file and sandpaper.

Next, cut the four shelves to final length on the miter saw. Test-fit the shelves between the two sides, and mark the width in relation to the curve of the sides, as shown (page 53).

Set your jigsaw's blade to the angle that matches the line, and rip each shelf to width. Clean up each cut as necessary with a block plane or a rasp and sandpaper.

Next, mark the placement of the pocket holes on the bottom of each shelf, 3/4" in from each long edge. Set the jig for 3/4"-thick material, and make a few practice holes in scrap material. When you feel confident, line up the mark on the shelf with the mark on the jig as shown (page 53), secure the shelf in the jig, and drill your pocket holes using the bit pro-

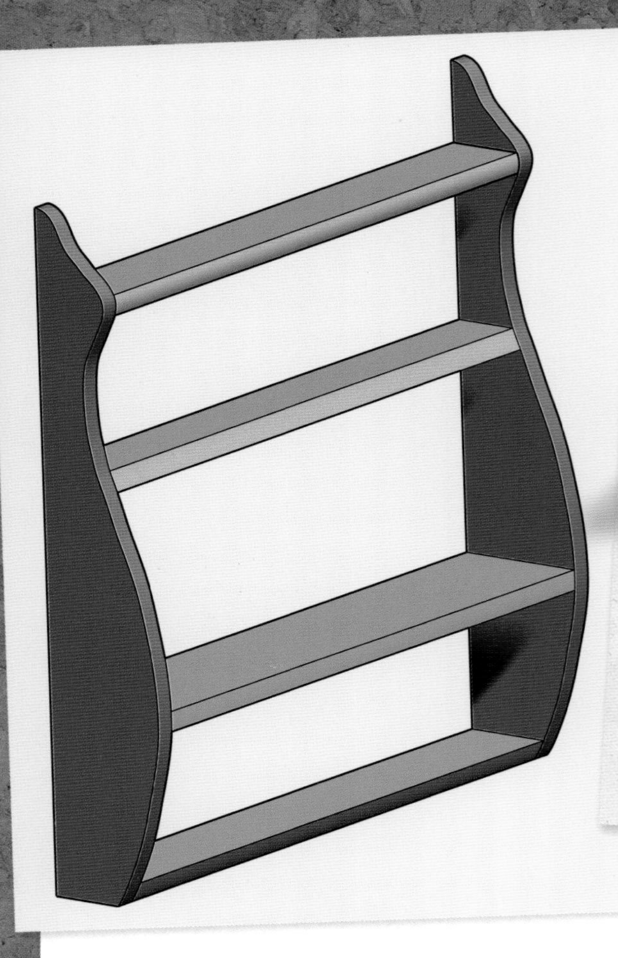

PARTS LIST

NO.	PART	STOCK	THICKNESS X WIDTH X LENGTH INCHES	MILLIMETERS	COMMENTS
2	sides	pine	$\frac{3}{4} \times 4\frac{7}{8} \times 25\frac{1}{4}$	19 × 107 × 641	
4	shelves	pine	$\frac{3}{4} \times 5\frac{1}{4} \times 23$	19 × 134 × 584	trim to fit

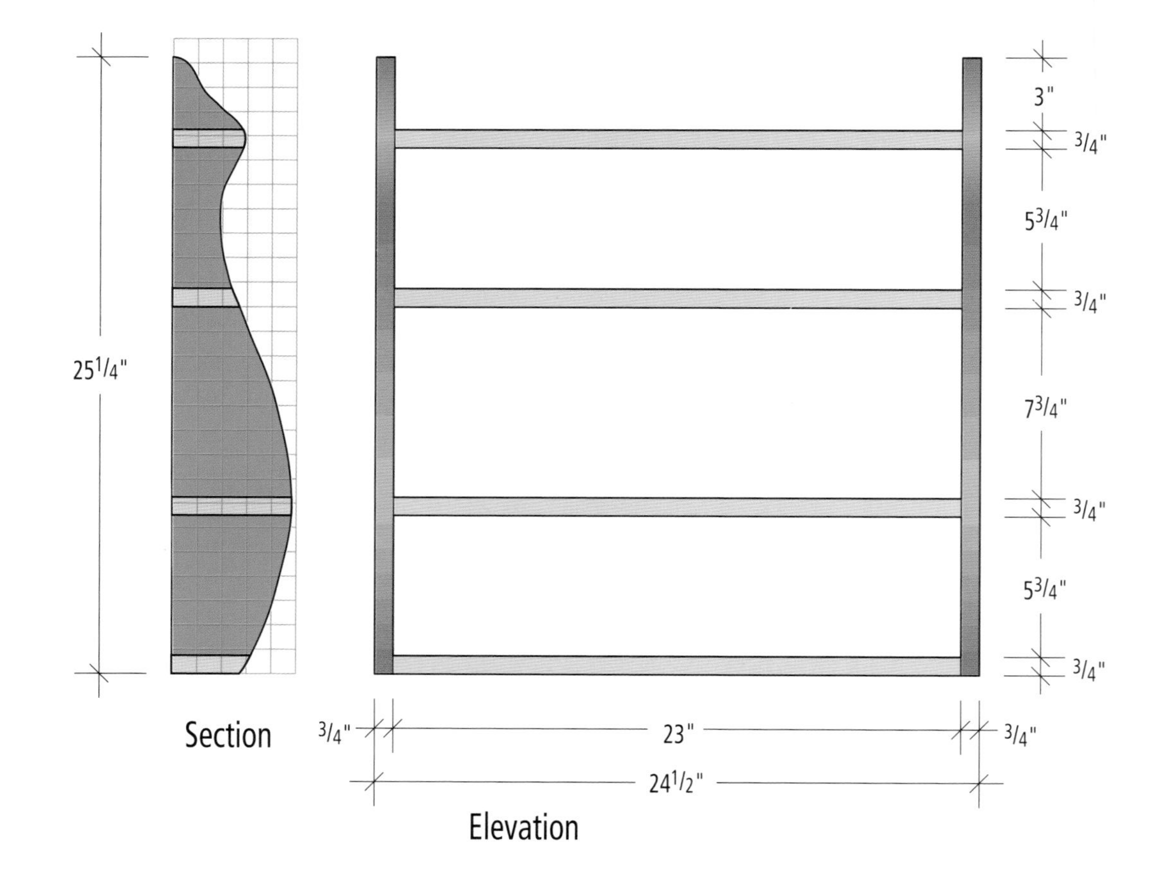

After transferring the pattern at the left to a piece of craft paper, use a craft knife to trace the pattern onto the side pieces. This will give you an easy line to follow with the jigsaw.

Use double-sided tape and clamps to keep your side pieces firmly together as you make your relief and curve cuts.

Fit the shelves against the two side pieces, and carefully mark the width in relation to the curve of the side. Then cut with your jigsaw.

vided in the kit. For the best result, keep the angle of your drill in line with the angle of the hole, and squeeze the trigger while the bit is at the top of the hole to allow it to get up to speed before making contact with the wood. Now drill the remaining fifteen pocket holes.

Before assembly, sand all the parts to #180 grit (stop at #120 if you plan to paint).

Using a scrap piece of material as a clamping block to help secure the shelf to the side as shown at far right, clamp the top shelf to the top of one side and drive pocket screws through the two pocket holes and into the side, using the driver provided in the kit. For the best result, set your drill on a low speed and clutch setting, to help avoid stripping the screws.

Now, attach the three remaining shelves to that side. Then attach the other side to the unit.

As shown, the whale tail shelf has three coats of brushed-on amber shellac. Sand between your coats with #320-grit stearated paper. Wipe off the dust with a tack cloth, and add a couple of coats of aerosol lacquer before attaching hangers to the back.

After securing the board firmly in the jig, squeeze your drill's trigger and allow it to get up to speed before drilling into the wood.

An offcut makes a handy clamping block to help you keep the shelves in place as you drive the pocket screws.

HALL BENCH

PROJECT 5

BY ROBERT W. LANG

Don't make the mistake of thinking you need a lot of tools and machinery to get started in woodworking. While it's certainly nice to have a jointer, planer, table saw and router, the only power tool I used to make this bench was a jigsaw.

We designed this project around available sizes of common lumber and put it together with a simple but strong method: nails and cleats. To add visual interest to this simple design, the ends are thicker than the front, back and top, and all of the joints are offset. This creates lines and shadows at the intersections. It also takes some of the pressure off your precision – if your measurements are slightly off no one will ever know.

Because I planned to paint this piece, I decided to use inexpensive material – #2 pine. I used 2 × 12 dimensional lumber for the ends, and 1 × 12 and 1 × 10 for the rest. If you want to use a clear finish to show the wood grain, you might want to upgrade to clear hardwood. Spend some time picking your material. You want the straightest pieces you can find with the fewest knots and other defects.

The shortest piece of 1 × 12 I could buy was 4' long. This length allowed me to cut between knots to get a clear piece for the top. I used the extra to make the 3/4" × 3/4" cleats that hold the front and back panels to the ends. I cut the top 1/8" shorter than the front, back and bottom to provide clearance when it opens and closes.

The two end pieces and the front and back panels were left at their full width; only the top and bottom need to be ripped to finished size. After cutting the ends to length, I marked out the feet at the bottom, made the cuts with the jigsaw, and cleaned up the saw marks with a rasp. I then used my combination square to mark the position of the front and back panels. I placed the panels against my marks as shown in the photo at right to determine the exact location of the cleats.

When I was sure that my layout marks for the top edges of the front and back panels were 1" below the top of the ends, I cut the cleats to length, allowing space for the bottom. I then put glue on the cleats

I used the front and back panels as gauges to locate the cleats that hold them to the ends. This avoids measuring errors.

PARTS LIST

NO.	PART	STOCK	THICKNESS X WIDTH X LENGTH INCHES	MILLIMETERS	COMMENTS
2	ends	pine	$1^1/_2 \times 11^1/_4 \times 16$	38 × 286 × 406	2 × 10
2	front & back	pine	$^3/_4 \times 9^1/_4 \times 27$	19 × 235 × 686	1 × 10
1	top	pine	$^3/_4 \times 10^3/_4 \times 26^7/_8$	19 × 273 × 683	cut from 1 × 12
1	bottom	pine	$^3/_4 \times 7^3/_4 \times 27$	19 × 197 × 686	cut from 1 × 10
4	cleats	pine	$^3/_4 \times ^3/_4 \times 8^1/_2$	19 × 19 × 216	

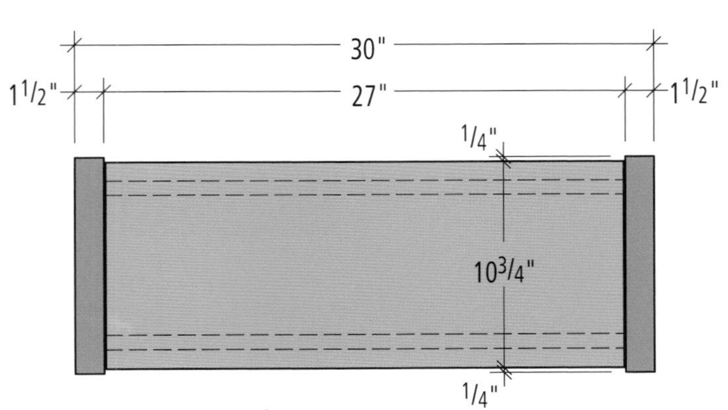

Plan

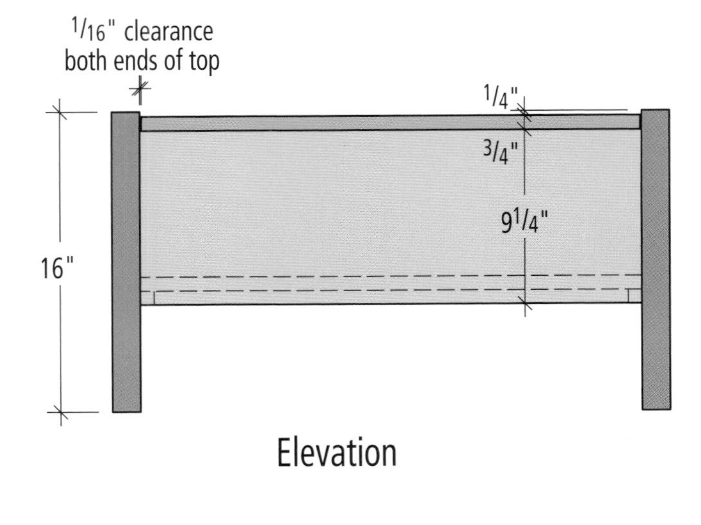

Elevation

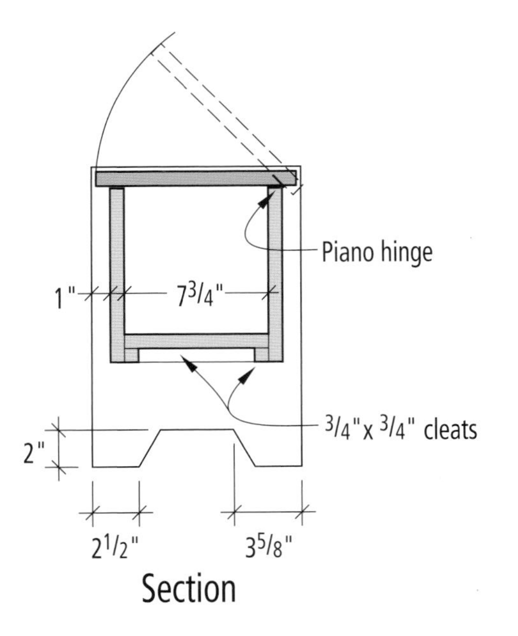

Section

After marking the location of the front and back, and the height of the top, I glued and nailed the cleats in place on the sides.

Planning a logical sequence for assembling the parts is important. I attached the front and bottom together and glued and nailed them to the ends as a single unit.

and nailed them to the end panels. While the glue was drying, I glued and nailed the bottom to the lower edge of the front panel. I then put this assembly on one end panel, gluing and nailing it to the cleat using 3d finish nails. Before putting the back panel on, I attached the other end.

I then placed the box face down on my bench and attached the back panel, using a couple of clamps to keep the assembly square and lined up with my pencil marks as shown in the photo (lower right). After setting the heads of the nails below the surface with a nail set, I was ready to attach the top to the back panel with a piano hinge.

With the top overhanging the back panel, I had room to surface mount the piano hinge. I used an awl to make pilot holes for the screws, and attached the hinge with just a few screws at first to be sure it opened and closed properly. Then I removed the screws and hinge and got the bench ready for paint.

I eased all the edges with my block plane and a rasp, then sanded with 100-grit paper to remove milling marks. If you use a random-orbit sander, stay away from the inside corners where the front and back panels meet the ends. If you get too close, the edge of the sanding disc can dig in. It's better if you stay an inch or two away with the sander, and work into the corners by hand.

I primed the bottom of the hinged top and the bottom edge of the ends first. When this had dried, I put a screw into the end of each foot to hold the ends off the surface while I painted the rest of the bench.

To get the back piece positioned exactly where I wanted it, I used a couple clamps to pull the parts into alignment.

PIANO HINGES

There are two important things to remember when setting hinges. The first is that you need to place the hinge exactly where you want it for it to function correctly. The second is that you want the screws that keep it in place to stay there forever, or at least as long as possible. The piano hinge on the hall bench is relatively easy to put in place, and the number of screws will give you plenty of practice, as well as some insurance if you don't get the first few in properly.

The simplest and one of the most accurate ways to locate the hinge is to arrange the top and the chest in a way that will let you put the hinge in place without trying to overcome the law of gravity.

Put the lid upside down on your Workmate, then place your assembled bench over it. You'll need to let the sides of the bench hang over the top of the Workmate. Once you have both parts in place, line them up where they will be after you've installed the hinge, as shown above.

Piano hinges are usually sold in 1' increments. You can either use a 24" hinge and leave equal spaces on each end, or you can use a 36" hinge and cut it to fit. To cut the hinge, use a Sharpie marker to mark a cut line, and cut the hinge with a hacksaw or with a metal-cutting blade in the jigsaw. With either method, you need to clamp the hinge securely to your bench to make the cut. You don't need to fill the space exactly, you should cut the hinge a bit smaller than the opening.

Put the hinge in place with the leaves of the hinge flat on the two pieces of wood. Hold the hinge in place with one hand, and use an awl (as shown above) to make a mark in the center of two or three holes.

The hinge is held in place with small screws, so you don't need a big hole to get them started. You also don't have the space to get your power drill in position to make a vertical hole, centered in the opening of the hinge.

If the holes for the screws are off-center, the beveled underside of the screwhead will move the screw as you tighten it.

When you attach the hinge, put two or three screws in one leaf, make sure the hinge is still in position, then put a few screws in the other leaf. This lets you check to see if the hinge will work the way you want it to before putting in all of the screws. If you've made a mistake, you can remove the screws, adjust the position, then reattach the hinge with screws in different holes. You'll find it's difficult to move a hole.

Once you're happy with the way the hinge operates, make the rest of the pilot holes and drive the remaining screws. You'll face the same problem with driving the screws you had in making the holes – there isn't room to use your cordless drill without the chuck rubbing on the wood.

Even though there are a lot of screws to drive, if you have a good pilot hole, they will be easy to drive by hand, especially if you used softwood. If you used a hardwood, it will be more difficult. You might want to lubricate the screws with paraffin or another wax to make the screws easier to drive. Think of this as skill-building practice. Make a few holes, drive a few screws, and compare the results with the last round.

You'll notice (above) that I put the hinge on before I painted the bench. Once I had the hinge working properly, I took it back off to paint the bench, then put it back on after the paint had dried. This may seem like a waste of time, but there's a good reason to do it this way.

If I had to make any adjustments that involved removing some wood, or if the top rubbed against the sides as the hinge opened and closed, I wouldn't be ruining the paint job. Repainting to cover damage would be a much greater waste of time.

SHAKER SHELVES PROJECT 6

BY MEGAN FITZPATRICK & GLEN HUEY

Basic skills are all it takes to create this graceful set of shelves, so with this project we'll teach you a few clever tricks to draw arcs without a compass, and to straighten twisted boards – which is often a problem when working with wider pieces of wood.

This modified Shaker design, downsized from a set of creamery shelves, is adapted from a Shaker Workshops catalog. To ensure our 3/4"-stock would not bow under the weight of even the heaviest items, we decided to make these shelf pieces a bit shorter than those on the company's web site (shakerworkshops.com).

Many home centers carry only pine, poplar and oak (you may also find maple or aspen, depending on your region). We decided on oak because we think it has the best natural appearance.

One of the biggest challenges you'll have with this project is finding wide boards that are straight and flat ... and that remain straight and flat after you cut them to size. Take time to look through the racks for the best boards – and if at all possible, avoid shrink-wrapped boards, no matter how pretty. You'll need two 6' and one 4' 1 × 12s (or one 10' and one 8' length). You'll also need a 6' length of 1 × 4 for the supports.

Once you're back in the shop, your first step is to cut the sides to length on your miter saw. If you have a 10" miter saw, your crosscuts on the sides (and shelves) will be a two-step process because the diameter of the saw blade limits the width of the cut. You'll need to first cut on one side of your board, then flip it over and carefully line up the kerf with the saw blade before completing the cut.

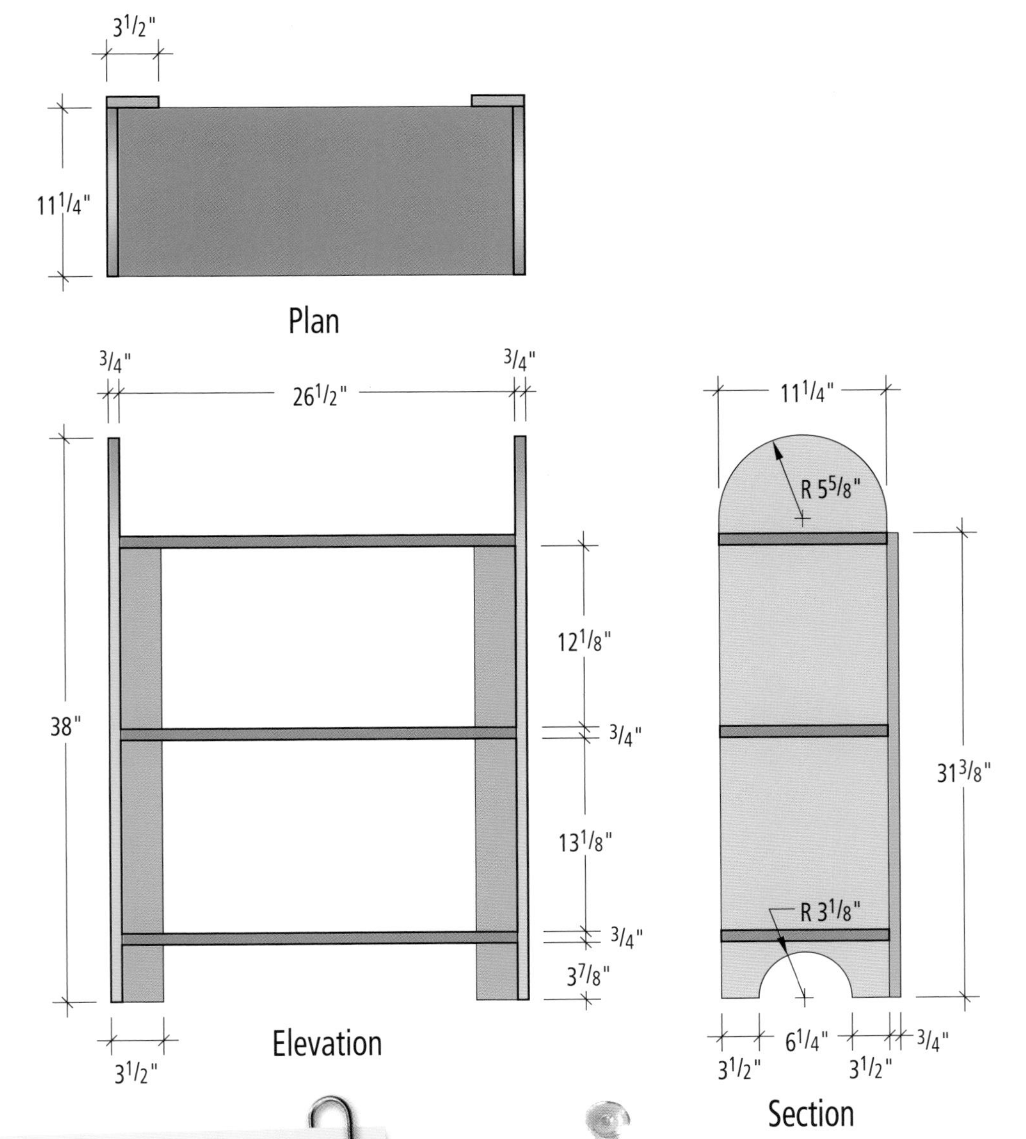

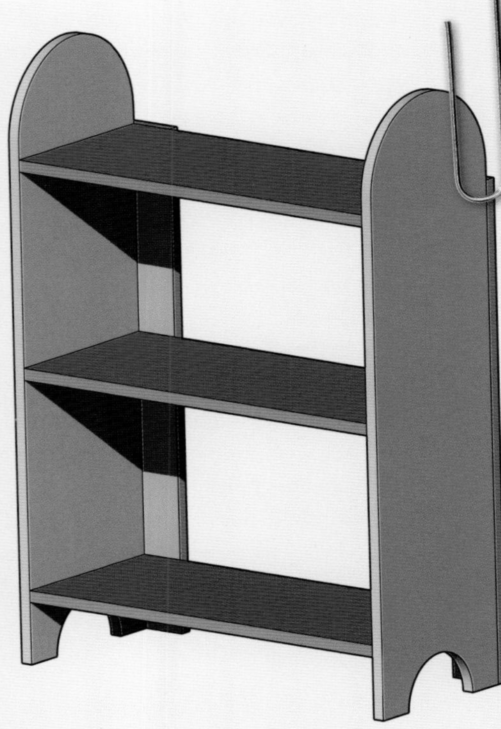

PARTS LIST

NO.	PART	STOCK	INCHES (THICKNESS X WIDTH X LENGTH)	MILLIMETERS
2	sides	oak	$3/4 \times 11^1/4 \times 38$	19 × 286 × 965
3	shelves	oak	$3/4 \times 11^1/4 \times 26^1/2$	19 × 286 × 673
2	supports	oak	$3/4 \times 3^1/2 \times 31^3/8$	19 × 89 × 797

Because the wood for the sides and shelves is $11^1/_4$"-wide and your miter saw is likely a 10" model, you'll have to cut the pieces in two steps. Measure and make the first cut. Then flip the board over and line up the saw blade to the existing kerf, and make the second cut.

A thin piece of scrap, a nail and a drill are all it takes to make this simple compass jig.

Now, you're ready to lay out the arched top and cutout at the bottom. Align the top edges of the sides and stick the faces together with double-stick tape to keep them from slipping, then clamp both pieces together flat to your workbench. Now, measure across the width to find the center of your board, and make a mark. That measurement is the same distance you'll measure down from the top edge to mark the intersection of the two points ($5^5/_8$" unless you've resized the plan, or used different-sized stock). This point is where you'll place your compass point to draw the half-circle arch across the top.

And if you don't have a compass, it's no problem. It's easy to make a compass jig. Simply grab a thin piece of scrap and drive a nail through the middle near one end. Now, using the same measurement you already established to find the compass point (again, it's $5^5/_8$" on our plan), mark and drill a hole that distance from the nail, and stick a pencil point through it. Voilà – a compass jig.

You can use that same jig for the bottom arched cutout. Simply drill another hole $3^1/_8$" away from your nail. Set the nail as close to the center of the bottom edge as possible and mark the cutout arch. Or, mark the arch with a traditional compass.

Now use your jigsaw to cut as close to the lines as possible, and use a rasp and sandpaper to clean up the cuts. If you keep the pieces clamped together during this process, you should end up with nearly identical arches. If you're not confident in your jigsaw skills, practice making curved cuts on some scrap pieces before moving on to the real thing.

Now cut the shelves to length.

Set up your pocket-hole jig for $^3/_4$"-thick material. Mark the placement for three pocket holes on each end of each shelf, two of them $^3/_4$" from each long edge, and one in the center of the end. Drill the holes.

Cut the back supports to length, and sand all pieces to 150 grit before assembly (120 if you're planning to paint).

Now you're ready for assembly, and the second trick we promised. Lay one side flat on your bench and mark the location of the top shelf at both sides. You may not be able to line the shelf up with your marks because of cupping in the wide board; that's where the trick comes in. Position the back support (or any straight piece of scrap) along the bowed side of the shelf, if there is one, and use clamps to bring the edges of the shelf flat to the support or straight scrap. Slide the clamped unit to the layout lines, hold or clamp it in place then use screws to attach it. This trick will work to pull the bow from any of the shelves.

Attach all three shelves to both sides, straightening the pieces where necessary.

Now lay the assembly face down, line up the support with the top of your top shelf. Drill countersunk holes at the top shelf, at the bottom shelf, and at the inside edge where the support meets the middle shelf. Be sure to hold your drill at 90° to the sides; because you're drilling into 3/4" stock, you could easily drill through the side if you're not careful.

Attach the uprights with #8 × 1¼" screws (rubbing the threads on some wax will help them seat more easily). Pay particular attention at the top and bottom as the stock can easily split. If it does crack, stop your drill immediately – but don't panic. Just back the screw out a tiny bit, and the split will close up.

Finish the shelves with two coats of wiping varnish.

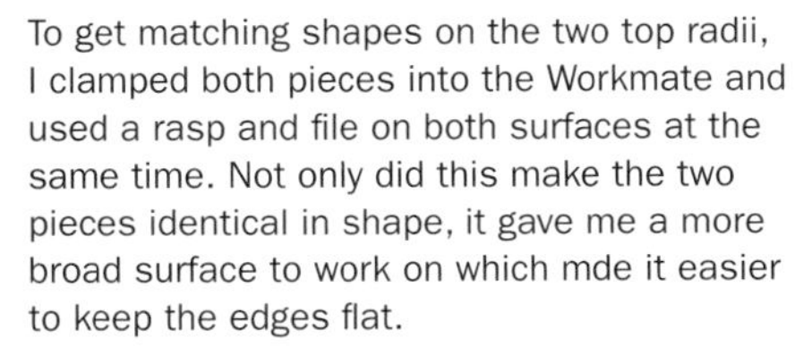

To get matching shapes on the two top radii, I clamped both pieces into the Workmate and used a rasp and file on both surfaces at the same time. Not only did this make the two pieces identical in shape, it gave me a more broad surface to work on which mde it easier to keep the edges flat.

You can pull a cup out of a board by clamping the piece to a straightedge and pulling it tight with clamps before screwing it down.

Make sure your drill is at a 90° angle to the most narrow stock through which you're drilling – in this case, the 3/4" edge of the side beneath the support.

MUD ROOM BENCH PROJECT 7

BY DAVE GRIESMANN

When I was shopping at my local home center for the material for this project I had three words in mind. "No gluing up!" So with that I set out to find 11"-wide lumber for the seat and legs. As luck would have it, they carried lumber 12"-wide × 96", so I was set.

This simple Shaker-inspired bench is a great project because it requires only four pieces of wood, but still provides a terrific place to stop and remove muddy shoes before entering the house. The top and two legs all come out of the 12" × 96" board, but I needed another board 3"-wide × 48"-long for the stretcher. I also needed a 3/8" oak dowel to make some plugs to hide screws.

The first thing is to cut the 12" wide board into three pieces using the miter saw. Cut two pieces at 15 1/4" in length for the legs and the other at 54" for the seat. Then cut your 3"-wide board to a length of 44" for your stretcher.

Twelve inches was wider than I needed for the legs and seat (and more often than not the factory edge on a board from the store can use a little help), so I ripped the three 12" pieces down to 11" in width. You can use a circular saw or jigsaw (see "Rules for using the tools").

Once you have the pieces cut to size

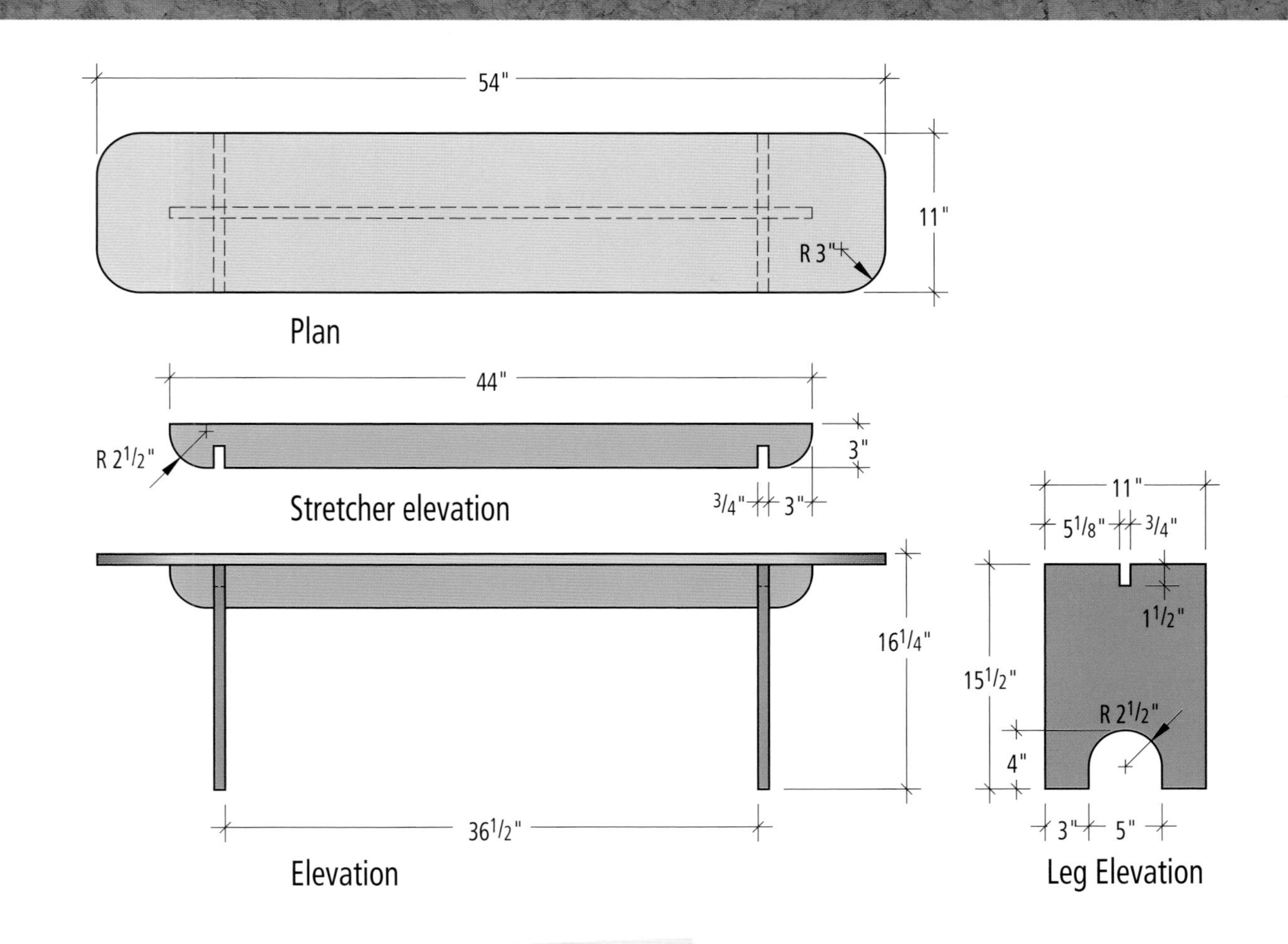

PARTS LIST

			THICKNESS X WIDTH X LENGTH	
NO.	PART	STOCK	INCHES	MILLIMETERS
1	seat	oak	$^3/_4 \times 11 \times 54$	19 × 279 × 1372
2	legs	oak	$^3/_4 \times 11 \times 15^1/_2$	19 × 279 × 394
1	stretcher	oak	$^3/_4 \times 3 \times 44$	19 × 76 × 1118

you are able to lay out the location and sizes for the radii on the the corners of the seat and on the bottom edge of the stretcher, as well as the cutout in the legs that give the bench a more elegant look (and make it easier for the bench to sit level on the floor). Last of all are the notches in the stretcher and legs to lock those pieces together. Start with the round shapes. You can use a circle template or compass to lay out a 2½" radius on the bottom corners of the stretcher. Then lay out a 3" radius on all four corners of the seat. If these aren't tools that you have in your shop, you can use any convenient round shape in your shop to mark out an attractive shape.

Now turn your attention to the legs. Using a combination square, draw a line 4" up from the middle of the bottom of the board. This is to mark the highest part of your circle cutout. Using a drafting compass lay out a 2½" radius circle with the top of the circle at the end of the 4" line you just drew. To complete this layout, draw a line from each side of the circle down to the bottom of the board. Once you have this arch layout complete, repeat the process on the other leg.

Using your jig saw cut out the arches and radii, making sure to cut on the waste side, leaving your line. Once that is completed use your palm sander and finish the cuts by sanding to the line.

If you don't have a drafting compass or circle template, don't hesitate to substitute the bottom of a coffee can or a spool of fishing line. As long as it looks good to your eye, it works!

After marking the 5"-diameter circle and extending the marks down to the bottom of the legs, use your jigsaw to cut out the arches on both legs. Take your time in the curve. It's easy to cut outside your line.

Cleaning up the cuts on the radii is fairly easy with a random orbit sander. Make sure you keep the pad perpendicular to the face of the board or you'll round over the edges. The sander won't work on the inside of the arches. You'll have to resort to a rasp and file to clean up those cuts.

Depending on your comfort leve with the jigsaw, cutting the mating notches for a tight fit can be tricky. You may want to cut the second notch by hand (I'm using a coping saw in the photo above). This allows you to sneak up on a tight fit.

Even though a long-grain to long-grain glue joint is stong, a handful of biscuits help reinforce the joint where the stretcher attaches to the seat (left). With the biscuit slots cut, add some glue and clamp the stretcher in place (above). If you've never tried wooden handscrews, you might be surprised at the amazing number of applications they have in your shop.

The next step is to lay out and cut the interlocking notches in the stretcher and legs. Layout a $^{3}/_{4}$" × $1^{1}/_{2}$" notch centered in the top of each leg. Then measure and mark out a $^{3}/_{4}$" × $1^{1}/_{2}$" notch 3" in from each side of the bottom of your stretcher.

Again using your jigsaw cut out the sides of each notch and cut a few straight relief cuts. A coping saw can help you finish cutting these notches and improve the fit. Use your palm sander and appropiate files to finish shaping the arch and the notches.

The next step is to attach the stretcher to the seat. I know I said no glue, but this is one place where it's a good idea. I also used biscuits to reinforce the glue joint. Line up the stretcher to the seat and mark several locations for biscuits. Make sure you stay away from the ends of the stretchers or the biscuit could show through at the radius. Once you have the biscuit slots cut, glue and clamp the stretcher into position.

When the glue dries, position the legs in place in the stretcher notches and turn the bench upright.

Because the legs and seat came from the same board and the grain is oriented in the same direction, we can use screws to attach the legs to the seat without any worry of wood movement causing splitting.

Use a $^{3}/_{8}$" countersink bit from the top of the bench to make the screw holes to attach the bench to the legs. Next cut four plugs from a $^{3}/_{8}$" oak dowel to glue and cover each screw hole. Once the glue dries, use a saw to cut the dowel plugs close to flush with the bench.

Using 150- and 180-grit sand paper on your palm sander; sand the entire bench. Take a rag soaked with water and wipe the bench down. This will raise the grain on the bench. When the bench is dry, sand it again using 180-grit sandpaper.

From here you're ready to finish however you wish. I finished my bench using an all-in-one mahogany stain from Minwax and then applied a few coats of wipe on poly.

I use a one-piece bit and countersink (lying on the bench) to make the clearance and countersink hole for both the screws and the plugs in one step. Just make sure you drill deep enough to allow the plug to seat $^{1}/_{4}$" below the surface.

The coping saw isn't my first choice for cutting the plugs flush to the top (it leaves more dowel than I'd prefer), but rather than go out and buy a flush-cut saw, I made do. Just a little more time spent on sanding and no one is the wiser.

COFFEE TABLE

PROJECT 8

BY GLEN HUEY

A coffee table is generally the focus of the living room. Sure the couch is the big comfortable sitting place, but the coffee table is the heart of the area. Where else do you prop up your feet? Where are the important magazines stored, to be pulled out when needed? The answer is your coffee table.

This particular table caught my eye because of the overall design. It is not too Country or Arts & Crafts and it will fit into either design quite well. It will also look proper within a contemporary setting.

The construction of this piece is uncomplicated. The top and shelf units are made of four individual pieces of lumber, which will help limit the total amount of wood movement versus using one solid glued panel. The legs are comprised of two pieces each and are attached to the top and shelf with screws. Add in the pieces that put the finishing touches on the sides and ends and this coffee table is ready for a finish.

And the finish could not be any easier to complete if it were painted, which would also be a nice look if you chose not to use the red oak as shown, but first things first.

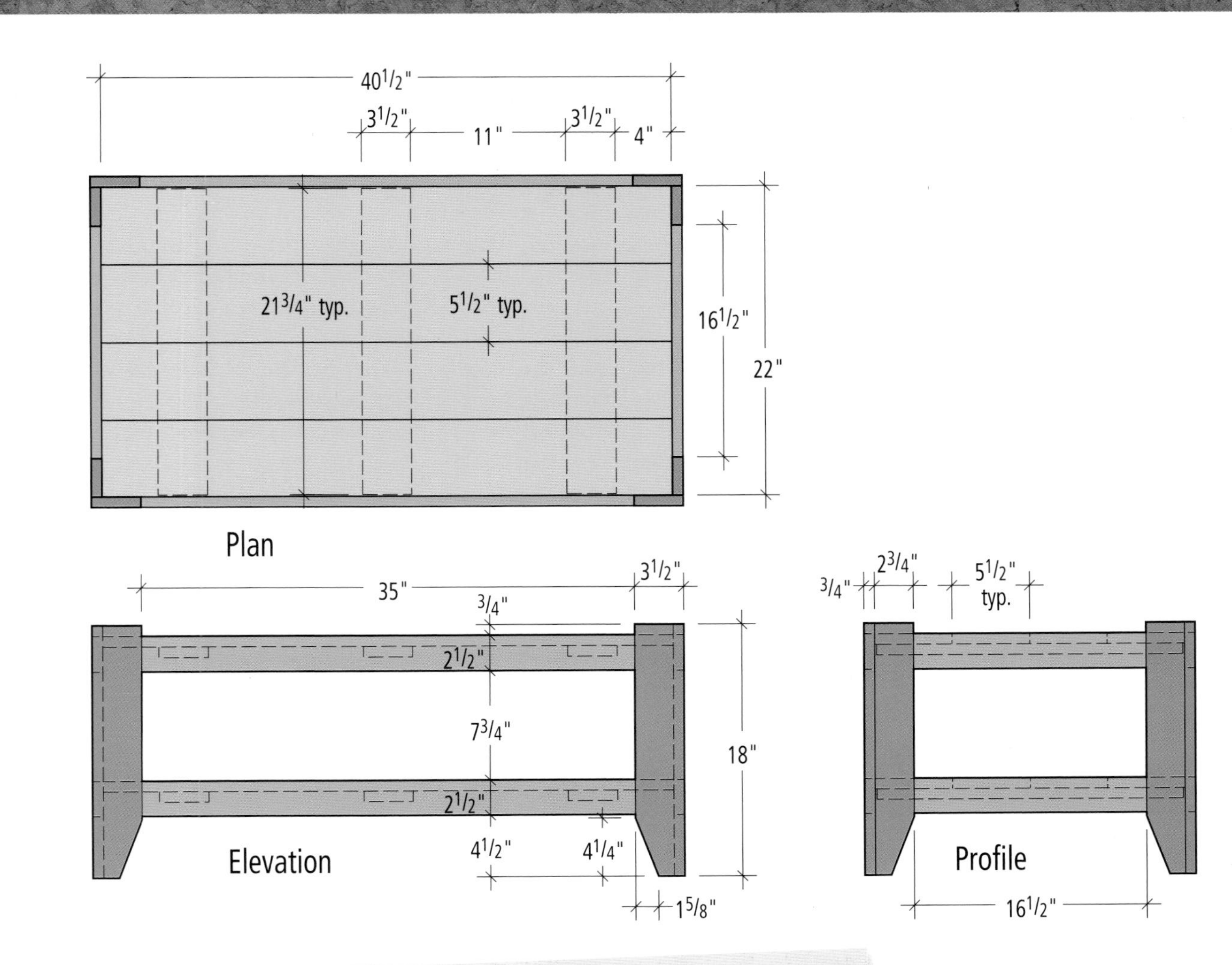

PARTS LIST

REF.	NO.	PART	STOCK	THICKNESS X WIDTH X LENGTH INCHES	MILLIMETERS
A	8	top & shelf slats	oak	3/4 × 5 1/2 × 40 1/2	19 × 140 × 1029
B	6	battens	oak	3/4 × 2 1/2 × 21 3/4	19 × 64 × 552
C	8	leg sides	oak	3/4 × 3 1/2 × 18 3/4	19 × 89 × 476
D	4	end rails	oak	3/4 × 2 1/2 × 16 1/2	19 × 64 × 419
D	4	side rails	oak	3/4 × 2 1/2 × 35	19 × 64 × 889
Screws		40 No. 8 × 1 1/4"			
		16 No. 6 × 1 1/4" pocket screws			
Nails		24 3d finish nails			

Making the Top and Shelf

Construction begins with the top and shelf pieces. Each of the two identical assemblies is made of four pieces of stock cut to the required length. Take the time to knock the sharp edges off of the pieces. This can be done with 100-grit sandpaper as shown on page 71 or if you would like a more pronounced rounding of the corners, use a hand plane to make the cuts on all the edges of each piece.

Position four of the top/shelf pieces on a flat surface, such as your bench top, with the best face down toward the bench and align the ends. Add clamps to help pull the pieces tightly together as well as to keep things from shifting as you attach the battens.

The battens are pieces of 1 × 4 that are cut a 1⁄4" less in length than the overall width of the assembled panel. Position three battens so they are about 2" from both ends and one is centered. To attach the battens use one screw (1 1⁄4" × No.8) directly in the center of each of the 1 × 6 pieces. Use a tapered drill with a countersink before installing each screw.

Having the screw located in the center of each piece will help to keep the wood stable with seasonal adjustments. The pieces will be allowed to move but the total movement is, in essence, cut in half because the pieces will only move from the center outward. If the pieces were screwed at both edges, the screws would restrict the movement and a crack or split might occur. Repeat these steps for the second assembly and set them aside for the time being.

A Leg Up

Cut the leg material to size and set four of the pieces to the side. The remaining four pieces need to have 3⁄4" taken from one edge. Mark the cut line and use a jigsaw to make the cut as close to the line as possible without crossing. Use a hand plane to straighten and square the cut edge to the line.

I made the angled foot cuts at the miter saw, though they also could be made with the jigsaw and cleaned up with a hand plane. In using the miter saw we can't set any angle past 45° (+ -). We need to make a steeper cut, so we need to base the cut off of the 90-degree setting. Position the saw to cut a 15-degree angle, place a temporary stop in place (bottom right photo) and set the cut to leave 2 1⁄8" of stock at the bottom edge of the leg. Make the cut on the four full-width pieces ,then set the stop so the

Knocking the corners off of all the edges will provide a shadow line as the pieces are place side by side. Don't try to find the joint - celebrate it!

Lay four pieces together as shown, aligning the ends, and add clamps to hold them in place. Attach the battens and the top and shelf are complete.

Patience is required when cutting the leg stock. Get close to the line and finish the edge with a plane.

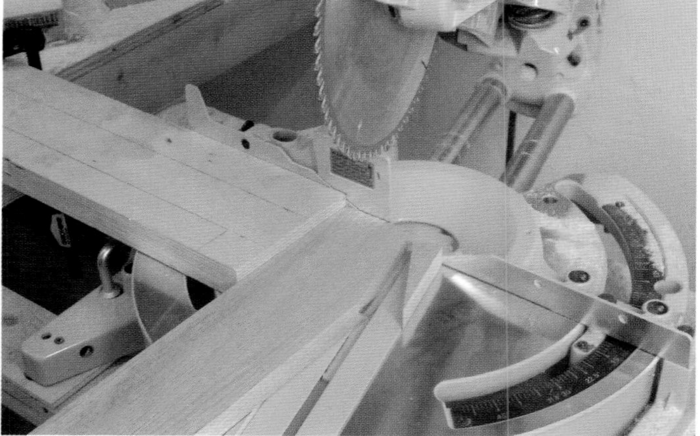

A set-up as shown will allow you to create the beveled feet whether you have a sliding compound miter saw or simply use a miter jig with a hand saw.

A strong glue joint and the correct orientation of the legs is important.

Stack the pieces of the table in any way you can to ready them for clamps. I found a neat way to use soda cans.

cut is made at 1⅝" on the pieces that were ripped with the jigsaw.

After the legs are assembled, the idea is to have identical views while looking at either face. You'll notice that the difference in the layout of the two cuts is exactly ¾" which is the amount ripped off with the saw.

Add glue to the ¾" edge of the narrow blanks and clamp the leg assembly together. Make sure as you tighten the clamps that the pieces don't slip. A little trick I've learned over the years is to add a little playground sand to the glue before adding clamps. The sand keeps the pieces from sliding, but indents into the wood, so the joint will still pull tight. Repeat the steps for each pair of leg blanks and set the legs aside to dry.

Time to Assemble

Position the top with the face down and raise the unit off of the bench with a couple of ¾" scraps. Next you need to find a way to position the shelf so your hands can be free to position the legs and add clamps. You can get a friend to help or think outside the box and find a special support system. The shelf should hit the legs 3½" above the terminating point of the angled cut. I found that two stacked soda cans worked great.

Set the cans at each corner and position the shelf, face down, on top of the can supports. Next, position the legs at each corner and add a clamp to each side. Once the clamps are in place, mark the location of the top edge of the shelf as it hits the

Mark the top or bottom edge of your shelf. You will need to get those cans out and precisely locate the shelf back in position.

Everything may be in position, but if your table is not square to the flat surface, you will find it extremely difficult to add the finishing pieces to the table.

legs. This is so you can correctly position the shelf after removing the cans.

Loosen the clamps slightly and slide the shelf upward. Remove the cans and tighten the clamps while repositioning the top at the marked lines. Do the same for the opposite end and you are ready to attach the legs to the top and shelf.

Before joining the two, make sure that the entire table, as it is to this point, is square to the bench. Tapping the unit with a rubber mallet or a hammer and a block of wood can make slight adjustments. Again, use the tapered pilot-drill and drive a $1^1/4$" × No.8 screw through each leg and into both the top and the shelf. Each leg will have a total of eight screws installed.

Before the clamps are removed, cut and fit the remaining pieces that complete the sides and ends. A snug fit is required. Use a pocket hole jig to drill a hole at the lower edge of each of the rails. Follow the manufacturer's instructions to create the pockets. After the pieces are fit and readied for the screws, attach the pieces to the leg assemblies with the recommended screws.

Drive nails into the side rails, three per side, and through the end rails into each piece that makes up the top and shelf. Two nails per piece — one $^1/2$" from each edge. Use a drill bit or begin the hole with the nail itself in the drill. The nails will allow for seasonal movement and help keep the wood flat because as the lumber moves, the nails will bend to and fro. Screws hold things fast and wouldn't allow for this natural happening.

Joining the legs to the top and shelf is easy with screws. Please don't use drywall screws, they will break, leaving you with much bigger problems.

The remaining pieces need a tight fit. Butt one end to the legs and mark the cut end to achieve that fit.

A pocket screw connection will hold the rails in place while you add the nails to complete the construction.

With a piece of the scrap wood and a plug cutter, you can make plugs that exactly match your project.

Knock down all sharp edge and corners before starting the staining process.

With these four finishing products you will complete your finish in a short time.

The construction is complete once you have filled the screw holes. The countersink part of the pre-drill leaves room for a 3/8" plug. These plugs can be purchased from the supply store, or cut from scrap material with a matching 3/8" plug cutter. Add glue in the hole and on the plugs and tap them in place with a hammer. Trim any additional material with a small saw or a plane and allow them to dry before finish sanding.

Wipe on, let sit, and wipe away. Repeat that twice, once with the stain and once with the oil and you are ready to add your top coat of shellac.

Preparing for a Finish

Before we look into that easy finish I mentioned, we need to get the table ready for finish. This involves sanding the flat surfaces with 120- and 150-grit sandpaper as well as rounding the ends of all the tops of the legs and the sharp corners. Use a file or rasp to ease the edges of the leg tops and carefully sand the areas smooth.

Once everything is sanded and ready, the staining is next. The staining process begins with a coat of Olympic Special Walnut wood stain. Use a clean rag to apply the stain. Rub on a heavy coating, allowing the stain to sit and penetrate the wood pores for about 15 minutes. Then wipe away any excess stain. This has to sit for at least 24 hours before moving on.

Once the stain is dry we move to the second coat of finish. This is a coat of Watco Danish Oil – Dark Walnut. Apply this in the same way as the stain. Put on a generous coat, allow the oil to seep for 15 minutes and wipe away any excess. Please take caution with these oily rags as they can become fire hazards if not properly treated. (Hand the rags on the edge of a garbage can and let them dry. Then they can be safely tossed into the garbage can.)

After the oil has dried for more than 24 hours we can apply the next coating — shellac. Rag a coat of shellac over the entire table. Try to not lap your application. Putting additional shellac over an area that already has a coat may produce lap marks, which will show in the final product. Keep a wet edge as you apply the top coat.

When the shellac is completely dry, a few hours later, lightly sand with a piece of No.0000 steel wool or a piece of 400-grit sandpaper. This will knock down any nibs left from the shellac. The final coat before using your table is a layer of paste wax. Rub it on, allow it to set and dry, then polish the surface to a warm sheen.

If you are like me, you will find a number of uses for a finish this easy. Move the table into your living room and add books — or maybe just your feet.

ROUND TABORET

PROJECT 9

BY DAVE GRIESMANN

Recently my wife put in a request for a small simple round-top table for our entry way. I did some checking around the internet and eventually saw an Arts & Crafts table that fit the general description, but our house has more contemporary furniture than that. So I thought about it for a while, changed a few features as well as the material (no oak in this one) and came up with a simple design that required minimal lumber and a chance to use my new trim router.

I knew with this piece I wanted to paint the base and have a natural finish top. Where I got lucky was finding one of the home centers that carried some maple boards. I picked up a $^3/_4$" × 6" × 96" maple board and then headed over to the racks with the the pine. All that was needed here was a $^3/_4$" × 6" × 96" board, a $^3/_4$" × 4" × 24" board and a $^3/_4$" × 3" × 108" board.

In my shop, I cut my 6" maple and pine boards into 22" lengths and edge glued them together to make two 22" × 22" blanks for my top and sub-top. The butt joint is one of the simplest of all woodworking joints, but when working with material that is already at its finished thickness, it can be a challenge to hold the edges of the pieces level with each other.

A simple way to solve this problem is to add biscuits to the edge joints. Though the biscuits aren't necessary for strength, they make it easy to align the pieces during glue-up. Use three biscuits at each joint, do a little sanding after the glue dries and you're done.

With the top and sub-top set aside to dry, I turned my attention to building the legs and stretchers of the table.

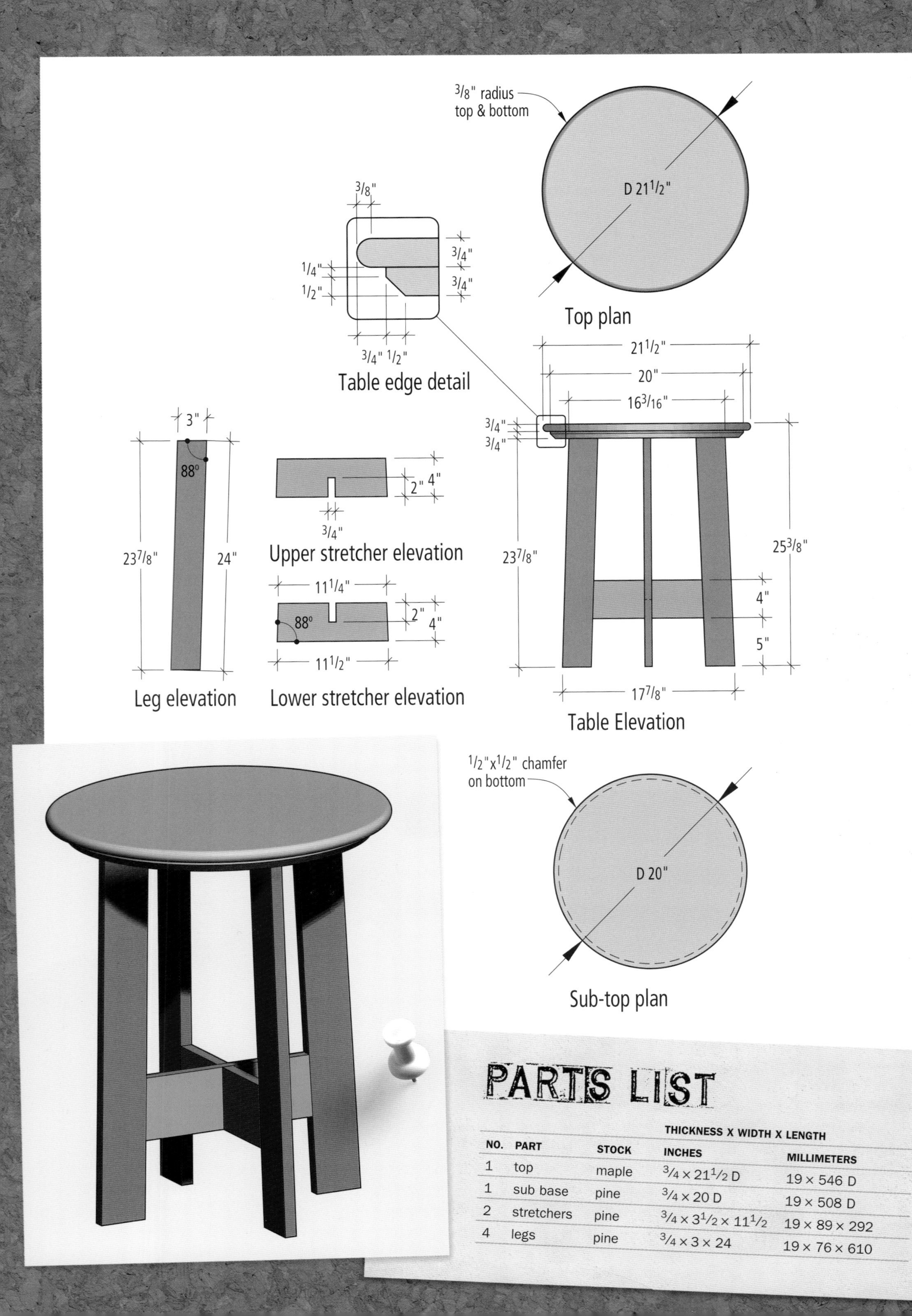

PARTS LIST

NO.	PART	STOCK	THICKNESS X WIDTH X LENGTH INCHES	MILLIMETERS
1	top	maple	3/4 × 21 1/2 D	19 × 546 D
1	sub base	pine	3/4 × 20 D	19 × 508 D
2	stretchers	pine	3/4 × 3 1/2 × 11 1/2	19 × 89 × 292
4	legs	pine	3/4 × 3 × 24	19 × 76 × 610

When cutting the half-lap notches, cut to the inside of the pencil lines, then nibble away the waste with successive cuts. A rasp and file will smooth the rough edges.

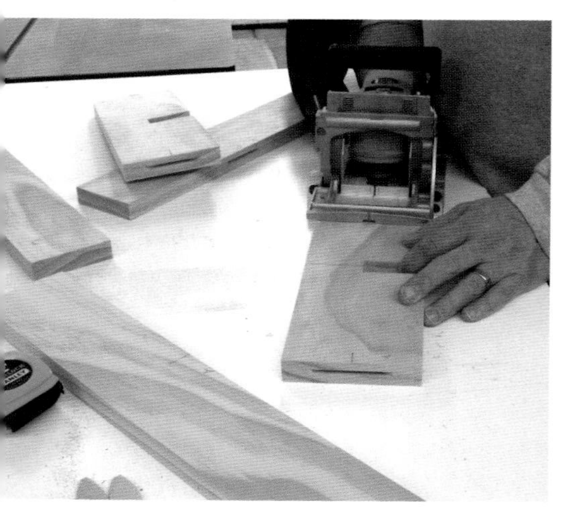

Biscuits attach the legs to the stretchers (or stretchers to the legs, depending on your point of view). While the slot in the stretcher is centered on the end, the slot in the leg is centered 7" up from the bottom.

If you look at the illustration on the previous page you can see that the legs of the table slant in from the floor to the top. To accomplish this I set my miter saw to cut at an 88° angle and cut the ends of my 3" wide boards. From here I slid the boards down 24" and make another cut at the same angle. These two cuts give me my four finished leg lengths and the legs slant perfectly.

Next are the two stretchers. Keeping my saw set at 88°, I take my 4" wide pine board and cut one end. I then flip my board over (end-for-end, keeping the same edge against the miter saw fence) and measure 11$^1/_2$" at the widest part of the board (don't measure from what will be the top of the stretcher, or it will end up too short) and make another cut at 88°. This gives me a stretcher that has two miters kicked in toward the top of the board. With that piece complete, I repeat the process on the second stretcher.

The two stretchers are going to have a half-lap joint at the center so the two stretchers will interlock. To create this joint, I lay out and mark a $^3/_4$" × 2" notch at the center of both stretchers — but with one notch at the top edge of one stretcher and the other at the bottom edge of the other stretcher.

From here I clamp one of the stretchers to my bench and using my jig saw I cut out the sides of the notch (leaving the pencil marks) and start cross cutting to remove the waste in between. From here I use my files and rasp to fine tune the joint so it is a tight fit.

The legs attach to the ends of the stretchers using biscuits. Mark and cut the biscuit slots on both ends of the two stretchers. Make the matching slots on the legs centered 7" up from the inside bottom of each leg.

While dry fitting the leg/stretcher assembly I noticed that I couldn't get good clamp pressure across the legs because of the slant of the legs. With that in mind I went back to my scrap and cut out four blocks that were 90° on one side and 88° on the other. I applied glue in each of the biscuit joint slots and on all four biscuits. When it came to putting the clamp on I used my scrap pieces to counter the slant of the legs and acted as if I were clamping all straight boards.

While the leg assembly was drying I went back to my sub-top and top and removed the clamps, removed any glue marks with my sander and was ready to begin to make my square tops round.

Starting with my sub-top, I used a tape measure and drew an X from corner to corner on the underside of my piece. This located my center point.

I then used a long piece of scrap and drilled a hole at one end to accept the tip of a pencil and measured in 10" on center

Clamping on a angle can cause the clamps to slip, messing up the procedure. A couple of scrap blocks cut at a complementary angle bring the clamping surface back to 90°.

Using a 1/2" high, 45 degree chamfer bit in my trim router, I carefully cut the bevel profile on the underside of my sub-top. This isn't a requirement for any building reason, but refines the underside of the table.

To finish the edge of the top I used a 3/16" roundover bit on both the top and bottom edges. A little hand sanding will blend the radius to the top and edge, removing the slight "edge" left by the router.

and drilled another hole for a nail. I hammered the nail into the center point of my sub-top just enough for the nail to stay in place but still be easily removed. From here I simply used this home made compass to draw the circle.

I clamped the sub-top to my bench and then, using my jigsaw, I carefully cut out the circle leaving the line inside my cut. (You will have to adjust your clamp several times so you can get the full circle cut). Switching between my files, rasps and sander I smoothed up the edge of the top, then added a chamfer to the bottom edge (top left photo).

While I was making circles, I went to work on making my top in the same manner as I made my sub-top except I adjusted my home made compass to be 10 3/4" (for a 21 1/2" diameter top), then added a roundover profile to the edge.

Next I unclamped the legs and cleaned them up using my sander (sanding to 120 grit), then I assembled the two halves. I centered the legs on my sub-top and marked the leg locations. I then marked an X at each leg location by drawing lines from corner to corner of my traced leg marks and drilled a small hole through the sub-top at each leg location.

Flipping everything over, I placed the sub-top back in place on top of the legs and then drilled 3/8" holes through the sub-top into the center of each leg about 1/2" deep. Then, after cutting a 3/8" dowel cut into four pieces, I applied glue to the holes and the dowels and tapped them into each leg. After the glue dried I cut the dowels flush and sanded the sub-top.

After final sanding the top to 120 grit I drilled through the sub-top and attached it to the top using four 1 1/4" × No.8 screws.

I applied several coats of wipe-on polyurethane to the maple top. Using flat black latex paint, I painted the sub-top and legs. I applied the paint using a foam brush and a small trim roller. Top it all off with a coat of paste wax on the top.

The legs are attached to the sub base using dowels whose locations are determined from below (left). Then holes are drilled and the dowels are put in place from above.

TIERED END TABLE

PROJECT 10

BY DAVE GRIESMANN

When I was drawing the sketches for this project I was reminiscing about the styles of furniture we had in the family as I was growing up. Back then the modern furniture had sharp corners, with straight or really drastic angles. But what I remember most was that all the kitchen appliances were burnt orange, harvest gold or avocado in color. With that in mind, you now know the reason behind my color choice in finishing this table.

Beyond the nostalgic coloring, I love the fact that this end table also doubles as a great location for storing books and for showing off pictures or other memorabilia, without taking up all of the top surface of the table.

Since I knew this piece was going to be painted I decided to build it using poplar. If avacado isn't your thing and you'd rather not paint, another option would be to use birch plywood, also available at your home center store. Iron-on veneer tape can be used to hide the plywood core and offer a more finished look to your project. But I was smitten by the avacado bug, so poplar and paint were my choices.

While I was at the home center choosing my lumber, I made sure to get lumber as close as possible to the finished sizes I needed. Meaning small stock for the bottom riser and wide stock for the rest.

Even thought I purchased the widest stock I could find, I still had to cut and glue up boards for the tops, side and risers. Whenever I needed to glue up a panel, I used biscuits to help align the two pieces during gluing. This also cut down dramaticaly on the sanding.

While my glued-up pieces were in the

PARTS LIST

NO.	PART	STOCK	THICKNESS X WIDTH X LENGTH INCHES	MILLIMETERS
1	top tier	poplar	$^3/_4 \times 18 \times 12^3/_4$	19 × 457 × 324
1	middle tier	poplar	$^3/_4 \times 18 \times 22$	19 × 457 × 559
1	bottom tier	poplar	$^3/_4 \times 18 \times 32^3/_4$	19 × 457 × 832
1	top divider	poplar	$^3/_4 \times 10 \times 10$	19 × 254 × 254
1	bottom divider	poplar	$^3/_4 \times 10 \times 20$	19 × 254 × 508
1	back	poplar	$^3/_4 \times 18 \times 20^3/_4$	19 × 457 × 527
2	riser sides	poplar	$^3/_4 \times 2 \times 30$	19 × 51 × 762
2	riser ends	pine	$^3/_4 \times 2 \times 13$	19 × 51 × 330
1	middle riser stretcher	poplar	$^3/_4 \times 2 \times 28^1/_2$	19 × 51 × 724

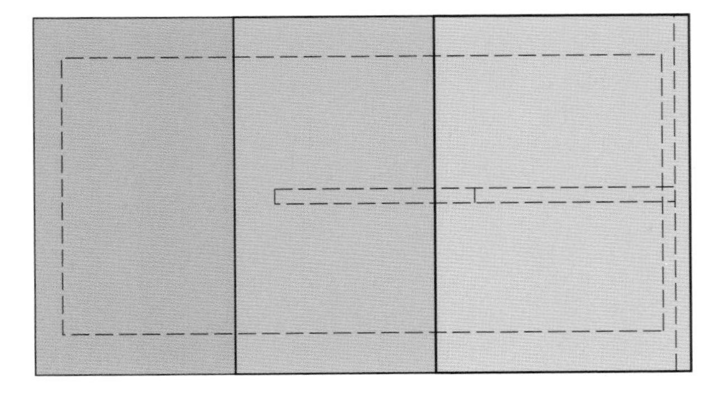

Plan

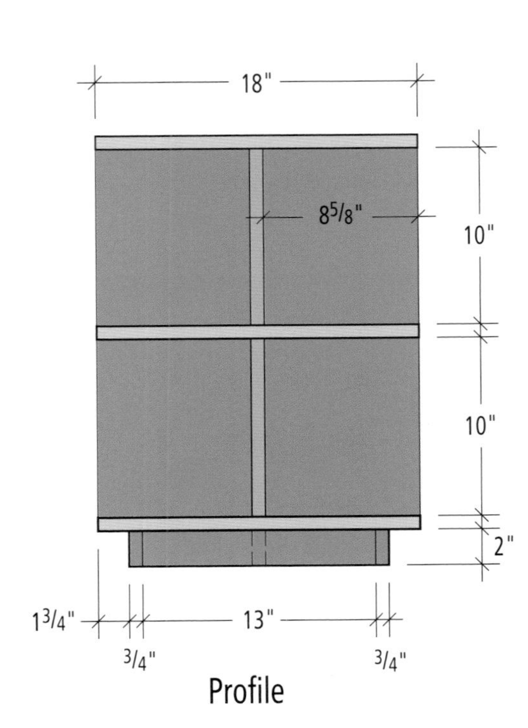

Profile

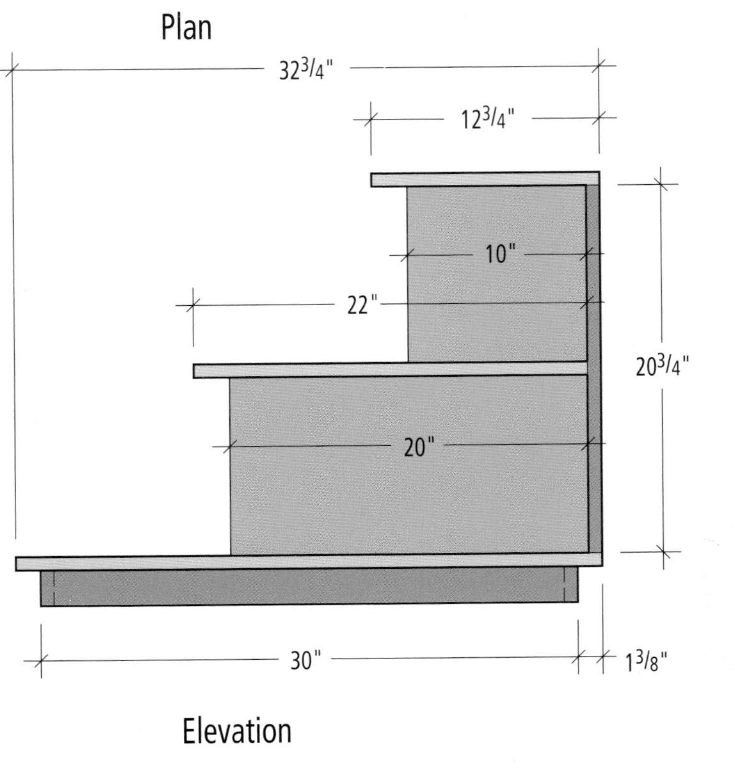

Elevation

clamps drying I turned my attention to building the bottom riser. I had purchased four pieces $\frac{3}{4}$" × 2" × 36" I ganged three of them using a clamp and my left hand to hold the three tight and squared up one end of all three.

Once I had the three pieces squared I ganged two of them together and cut them to 30" in length and the third piece to be $28\frac{1}{2}$". These will act as the two sides and middle stretcher of my riser. For the two ends of my riser I squared up one end of my fourth piece and cut it into two 13"-long pieces.

To assemble the riser frame, I used my pocket hole jig and screws. I drilled two holes on both ends of the two end pieces and on both ends of the center stretcher. Once I had everything aligned, I used $1\frac{1}{4}$"-long pocket-hole screws to assemble the riser.

Now I turned my attention back to my clamped up pieces. Once I had the clamps off I used a scraper and my random obiter sander with 80- and then 100-grit sandpaper to clean up any glue squeeze out and to flatten the pieces.

Once I had my boards flattened I cut my three tops, two dividers and my back to size using my jigsaw. I cut close to the lines and used my block place to clean up the edges.

With all the pieces cut to size I was ready to assemble the project. I gathered up my cordless drill, a box of square drive No.8 × $1\frac{1}{4}$" self-tapping deck screws, a couple of No.20 biscuits, my biscuit cutter, a square and a piece of $\frac{3}{4}$" × $\frac{3}{4}$" × 20" scrap. That's all that is needed to assemble this piece. (Well, that and bit of patience, since the process is a bit repetitive.)

Starting with the 18" × 30" bottom tier, I used my scrap piece to mark where the $\frac{3}{4}$" -thick back sits on top of the bottom. I also marked where the $\frac{3}{4}$"-wide × 20"-long bottom divider is centered on the bottom. With these two locations marked I pre-drilled the holes to attach the back and the bottom divider. I first attached the back to the bottom, then flipped the assembly onto its back and attached the bottom divider.

With the assembly still laying on its back, I marked on the back where the middle tier will attach, pre-drilling into the back. I also marked on the middle tier where the bottom divider will attach. Once I had this laid out I went ahead and

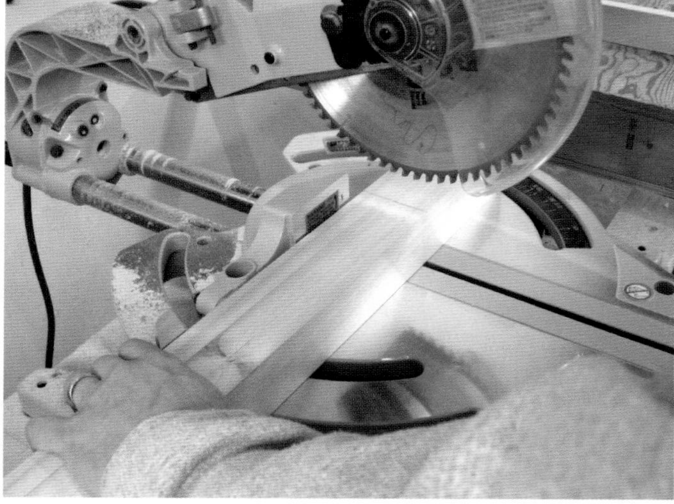

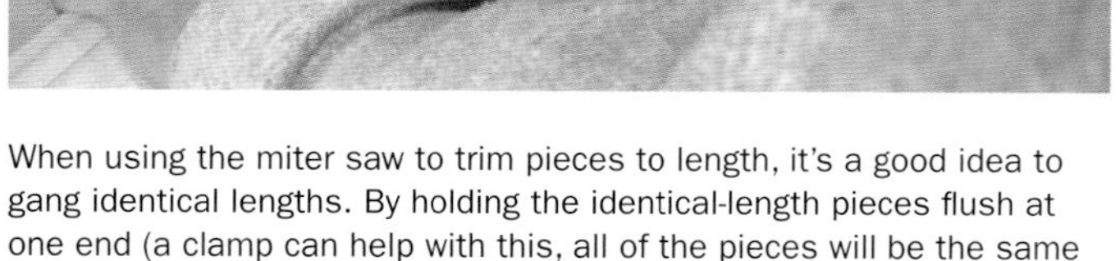

When using the miter saw to trim pieces to length, it's a good idea to gang identical lengths. By holding the identical-length pieces flush at one end (a clamp can help with this, all of the pieces will be the same length, avoiding problems during assembly.

Square cuts on the ends of the boards will ensure a square frame, but it's still a good idea to check for square as you screw the riser together.

You could use a square and ruler to lay out the locations of the back and bottom divider, but I find using a scrap of the actual pieces themselves gives me a more accurate representation of the pieces.

After marking the locations for the back and divider, I drill pilot holes for the screws through the top surface. Working from this side will guarantee the any blow-out from the drilling will end up on the bottom surface.

To keep the screws flush to the bottom surface, I first used a countersink bit at each hole location, then screwed the bottom tier tightly to the divider.

When cutting the biscuit slots in the middle tier piece, it's very important to keep the base of the biscuit jointer accurately located on your layout line. If the biscuit is not parallel to the line, the biscuit will not fit into both slots.

The last tier is screwed in place into the top edge of the back and the top edge of the divider. Pre-drilling is still important at this step, as is making sure your screw is driving straight (not at an angle) into the piece below.

I didn't use glue to attach the riser to the bottom for two reasons: Glue can cause problems with seasonal movement, and I wanted to finish the piece with the base detatched.

pre-drilled and attached the middle tier to the bottom divider. I then flipped the assembly onto the bottom tier and attached the middle tier to the back, again countersinking the screw heads.

Once the middle tier is attached, you won't be able screw up through the middle tier to attach the top divider. Instead, I used biscuits to attach it. I marked the 3/4" × 10" location of the top divider on the middle tier and its location in the middle of the back. I again pre-drilled the back, then marked two biscuit locations on the divider and middle tier pieces. I then set my biscuit jointer to cut No.20 biscuit slots and cut two slots in both pieces.

From here I used an acid brush and spread glue on the biscuits, and on the bottom of the top divider and tapped the divider into place on the middle tier. Lastly, I attached the back to the divider with screws.

We're almost to the end. To attach the top divider and top tier, I followed the same process to lay out the location of the divider on both the back and the top tier piece. The divider is again biscuited to the tier below and attached to the back by screws.

Because I'm painting my table, I went ahead and attached the top tier to the assembly using screws through the top. If you're staining you would be better off using biscuits to attach the top tier piece.

Even though I'm painting, I don't want my screws to show. So while the glue was drying, I filled the countersunk holes with paintable wood putty. After the putty dried I sanded it flush to the top surface.

The last assembly step is to attach my riser to the assembled unit. With the riser still loose from the table, I used my pocket-hole jig to drill three holes on the inside of both the side and the middle dividers. I then turned the piece on its side and marked an X from corner to corner to center the riser and then attached the riser to the bottom of the piece.

With just a little finish sanding, I was ready to apply my finish. I chose to stain the riser a dark walnut to give the table a feel of floating off the floor. I removed the riser and stained it separately. I applied three coats of avocado paint to the table. Then I reatteached the riser to the table.

The concept used to build this table also set my mind to thinking about building a tiered shelving unit to match. With the practice gained on this table, the shelf should be an easy project — someday.

OPEN BOOKCASE

PROJECT 11

BY A.J. HAMLER

Ah, wonderful plywood! Good quality oak is expensive. In fact, if you were to make this bookcase with solid 3⁄4"-thick oak you'd easily spend over $125 for the wood – probably more – at home center prices.

On the other hand, a single 4 × 8 sheet of 3⁄4" oak veneer plywood will create all the components for this project for about $40, with plenty left over for future projects. (You can also buy oak ply in 2 × 4 and 4 × 4 sheets.) As a bonus, plywood at home centers is generally far straighter and flatter than dimensional oak, which is prone to severe warping in the storage racks. Plywood has an unattractive edge, but we'll fix that with iron-on oak edge-banding for a finished appearance.

Can't handle a big sheet of plywood in your car? No problem. They'll cut it to a more manageable size for you on one of their big panel saws, killing two birds with one stone: Not only does it make transporting it home easier, but having the sheet ripped to width before leaving the store will save a lot of time and effort over doing it with a jigsaw. However, plywood is notorious for tear-out when crosscutting, so only have them do the ripping; crosscut the pieces to length yourself when you get home. Your best bet is to have them cut enough 10"-wide stock to create the four shelves and the six main vertical pieces, plus one 4' length each of 3 1⁄2" wide and 6 1⁄2" wide stock for the

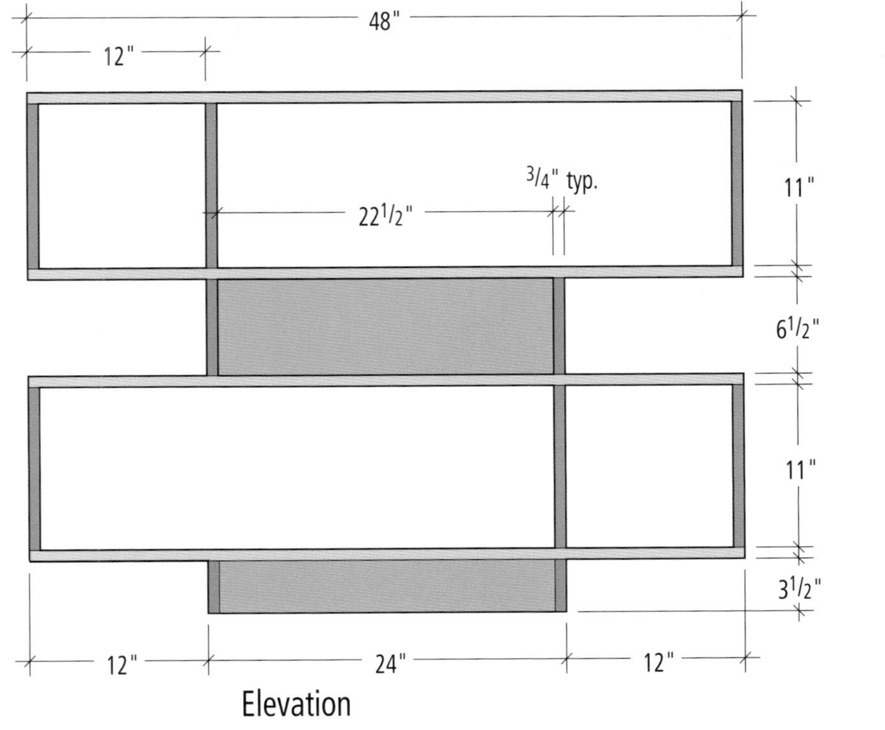

Elevation

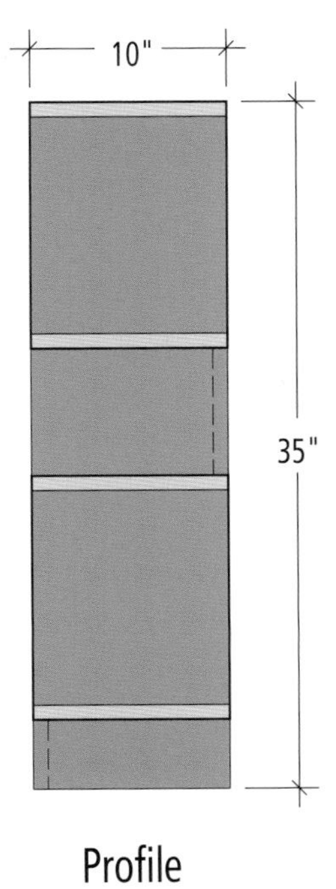

Profile

PARTS LIST

NO.	PART	STOCK	THICKNESS X WIDTH X LENGTH INCHES	MILLIMETERS
4	shelves	oak plywood	$\frac{3}{4} \times 10 \times 48$	$19 \times 254 \times 1219$
6	main verticals	oak plywood	$\frac{3}{4} \times 10 \times 11$	$19 \times 254 \times 279$
1	base front	oak plywood	$\frac{3}{4} \times 3\frac{1}{2} \times 22\frac{1}{2}$	$19 \times 89 \times 572$
2	base sides	oak plywood	$\frac{3}{4} \times 3\frac{1}{2} \times 10$	$19 \times 89 \times 254$
1	divider back	oak plywood	$\frac{3}{4} \times 6\frac{1}{2} \times 22\frac{1}{2}$	$19 \times 165 \times 572$
2	divider sides	oak plywood	$\frac{3}{4} \times 6\frac{1}{2} \times 10$	$19 \times 165 \times 254$

Oak iron-on edge-banding $\frac{3}{4}$" (19mm)

One face of a plywood sheet is typically better than the other. Orient components with face blemishes so they're not easily seen.

To prevent tear-out when crosscutting, score the cut line with a utility knife or razor blade.

base and divider sections. Leave the rest uncut for future use.

Although both faces of the plywood are oak, one side is usually better than the other. Sometimes, the occasional knot can be an interesting detail, but examine your components for undesirable surface flaws and orient them so they'll be less visible in the finished piece — such as the underside of shelves, or facing inward where they'll likely be hidden by books.

Measure and mark each of the 10"-wide pieces to length for the shelves and verticals, but before cutting, score along the cut line several times with a utility knife. This will help prevent tear-out as you cut. With the jigsaw's orbital action on the lowest setting for a cleaner cut, crosscut your pieces to length. Clean up the cut if necessary with a piece of sandpaper wrapped around a wooden block, but leave the edges sharp for now.

Cut carefully up to the cut line, with the jigsaw's orbital action on the lowest setting for a cleaner cut. When crosscutting, keep these less-attractive faces up — jigsaws tend to tear out on the top surface when cutting.

Do the same to cut the $3^1/2$" and $6^1/2$"-wide components of the base and divider sections to length. Depending on its capacity, you may be able to cut these narrower pieces on your miter saw. No scoring is necessary here, but use a piece of scrap underneath to prevent tear-out on the underside.

With all the components cut, organize and mark them with a pencil according to face appearance. Again, less attractive faces should orient either down, inward or to the back.

Getting the Edge

The only drawback of using plywood for furniture is that the raw edges don't match the oak faces, but you can correct that easily with oak edge-banding. Furniture manufacturers use huge, ridiculously expensive automated machines to apply hundreds of thousands of feet of edge-banding for furniture components. Fortunately, there's an easy, inexpensive home shop option for doing the same thing.

Iron-on edge-banding can be quickly applied — it comes with hot-melt glue already on the contact surfaces — and once trimmed will give plywood edges the look of solid wood. Oak edgebanding is readily available at home centers, usually in 25' rolls for about $6. You'll want to apply it to all visible edges, so you'll need about 30' for this project, plus a bit extra for trimming purposes, so you may have to buy two rolls. If you plan to use your bookcase against a wall, there's no need to put it on the back; for a freestanding bookcase, apply it to the rear edges, too.

Cut all the edge-banding pieces to length with scissors, allowing an extra inch on each end, but handle it carefully as it's easy to get splinters. Be sure to refer to the packaging for specific iron settings.

Edge-banding is quite thin, but you'll still want to apply it before assembly so all components go together flush. Hold the edge-banding in place with one hand while running the iron carefully along the length. Check frequently to be sure it's adhering and continue until the entire piece is securely attached. Mistakes are easy to fix: Just reheat with the iron and correct it. When cool, trim the ends flush with a utility knife.

Because plywood is slightly thinner than the nominal thickness — 3/4" ply is really about 23/32" thick — the edgebanding will overhang the edges a bit. This can be trimmed with a knife or a small block plane to almost flush. Take it down the rest of the way with a sanding block, but leave the edges sharp for now; we'll soften those edges after assembly. Put edge-banding on all components except the front edges of the center divider. We'll do that later.

Putting It Together

Assembly is easiest if you put the components together in sets, starting with the base section and working from the ground up. Line up the components so that the front piece is flush with the edge-

A miter saw makes short work of crosscutting the narrower piece. Put a piece of scrap beneath the workpiece to prevent tear-out on the underside.

An ordinary household iron can apply edge-banding quickly and easily. (Get permission *before* borrowing the iron for shop use.)

Since edge-banding is slightly wider than the plywood edge, trim the excess with a knife or a small block plane. If using a razor knife (left), keep the blade parallel to the wood's surface, or slightly canted edge-up. It's very easy to gouge the veneer if you get distracted. Sand edge-banding smooth and flush with a sanding block (above).

The type of plug you use determines how your project will look. The face-grain plug on the left (inset) will hardly be noticed; the end-grain plug on the right will add a contrasting detail. Put a small amount of glue in the countersunk hole with a nail or toothpick, insert the plug (left) and tap gently into place. Sand plugs flush with the surface when dry.

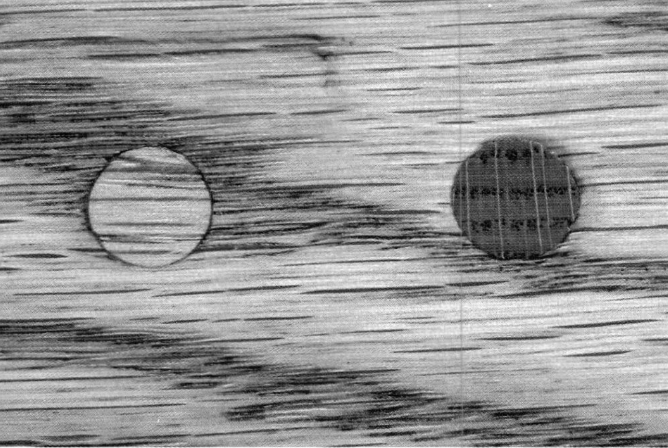

banded sides, and drill countersunk pilot holes at the screw locations. I use a combination drill/countersink that leaves perfect 3⁄8" holes above the screw head, just right to accept an oak plug that hides the screw. Plugs are available in a variety of wood species at your local hardware store or home center, or from any woodworking supply catalog. Plugs come in two types: end grain and face grain. End grain plugs accept stain more readily, making for a darker finished plug which can be a nice accent. For something more subtle (in fact, almost invisible) use face-grain plugs. Put a bit of glue in the countersunk hole, drop in a plug, set it in place with a few light taps from a hammer, and sand flush with a sanding block.

Note that the interior vertical pieces in the shelf sections are offset and line up exactly on one side with the base and divider sections, so center the finished base on the very bottom shelf and trace the outline on one side as a guide for locating the vertical piece in the bottom. Set the base aside and assemble the lower shelf section.

To attach the base to the bottom shelf section, flip everything upside down. I simply drove a few screws up through the base into the bottom of the shelf section, using the drill from my pocket-screw set for pilot holes. Measure the drilling depth carefully and wrap masking tape around the bit to mark the depth. Drill your holes, apply a bit of glue to the mating edge of the base, and screw it into place.

As with the base, use the assembled divider section to mark locations of the interior vertical piece. There's no vertical piece on the left side, so just drive screws up from underneath and plug them, but the vertical will limit access to the lower shelf unit on the right side. Solve this by driving screws at a 45° angle through the front and back of the divider section, using your pocket-hole bit to make the pilot holes. (That's why we didn't put edgebanding on the front of the divider section.) You'll find that this is easier to accomplish if you clamp the section together before drilling so that the parts remain aligned.

Before assembling, mark the locations of the vertical components so they can be lined up accurately.

Build each of the four sections of the bookcase – base, divider and the two shelf sections – separately, then assemble them.

To prevent drilling pilot holes too deeply (and risking drilling through the workpiece) measure the depth carefully, marking the drill bit with some masking tape.

When assembling the four sections, clamping them together will keep everything aligned when drilling and driving screws.

Repeat the process with the top shelf section. As before, you can drill and plug on one side, and screw at a 45° angle on the other. When completely assembled, cut edge-banding to fit the front edges of the divider section, and iron in place to hide the angled screws.

With the bookcase assembled, check for any bits of tear-out that may have occurred when crosscutting and fill with wood filler. Ease all the edges with fine sandpaper. Good oak plywood doesn't usually require a lot of sanding, but you may want to go over the whole piece for a uniform smoothness.

Stain the bookcase if desired – I used a golden oak stain on this one – and top it off with a few coats of satin polyurethane.

SHAKER SHELF

PROJECT 12

BY GLEN HUEY

In the 1989 edition of the Willis Henry Shaker auction of ephemera, woodenware and furniture, this Canterbury, New Hampshire, shelf immediately caught my eye. I've incorporated a few size and construction variations from the antique in my version, but this design is true to the spirit of the original.

You'll find a use for those scraps from earlier projects if you decide to paint this piece. Mixed woods are often found in antique furniture. Don't be afraid to try it (if you don't have enough scraps, head to the home center).

Building the drawer for this shelf is a new technique, but don't freak on me! It appears more complex than it is and your list of must-do projects will grow once this skill is in your arsenal.

Curvy Bottoms Add Appeal

Each side of the shelf has three curves or arc cuts. Each arc evolves from the previous arc, starting with the smallest radius at the lower, rear corner of each side.

Crosscut the sides to length and draw the pattern on the pieces. The size of each radius is called out on the illustrations and can be easily transferred to the side using a compass. You could also choose to lay out the curve on a piece of cardboard,

PARTS LIST

NO.	PART	STOCK	THICKNESS X WIDTH X LENGTH INCHES	MILLIMETERS
1	top	poplar	3/4 × 9 1/4 × 22 3/4	19 × 235 × 578
2	sides	poplar	3/4 × 7 1/4 × 17 1/2	19 × 184 × 445
1	top face rail	poplar	3/4 × 3 1/2 × 17 1/4	19 × 89 × 438
1	bottom face rail	poplar	3/4 × 2 1/2 × 17 1/4	19 × 64 × 438
3	internal rails	poplar	3/4 × 2 1/2 × 17 1/4	19 × 64 × 438
2	drawer sides	poplar	3/4 × 3 1/2 × 6 1/4	19 × 89 × 159
2	drawer front/back	poplar	3/4 × 3 1/2 × 15 3/4	19 × 89 × 400
1	drawer face	plwood	1/4 × 3 3/4 × 17 1/4	6 × 95 × 438
1	drawer bottom	plywood	1/4 × 6 1/4 × 17 1/4	6 × 159 × 438
1	case back	plywood	1/4 × 8 × 17 1/4	6 × 203 × 438
1	bed moulding	pine	9/16 × 2 1/4 × 48	14 × 57 × 1219
2	wooden knobs	1 1/2in (38mm) diameter		

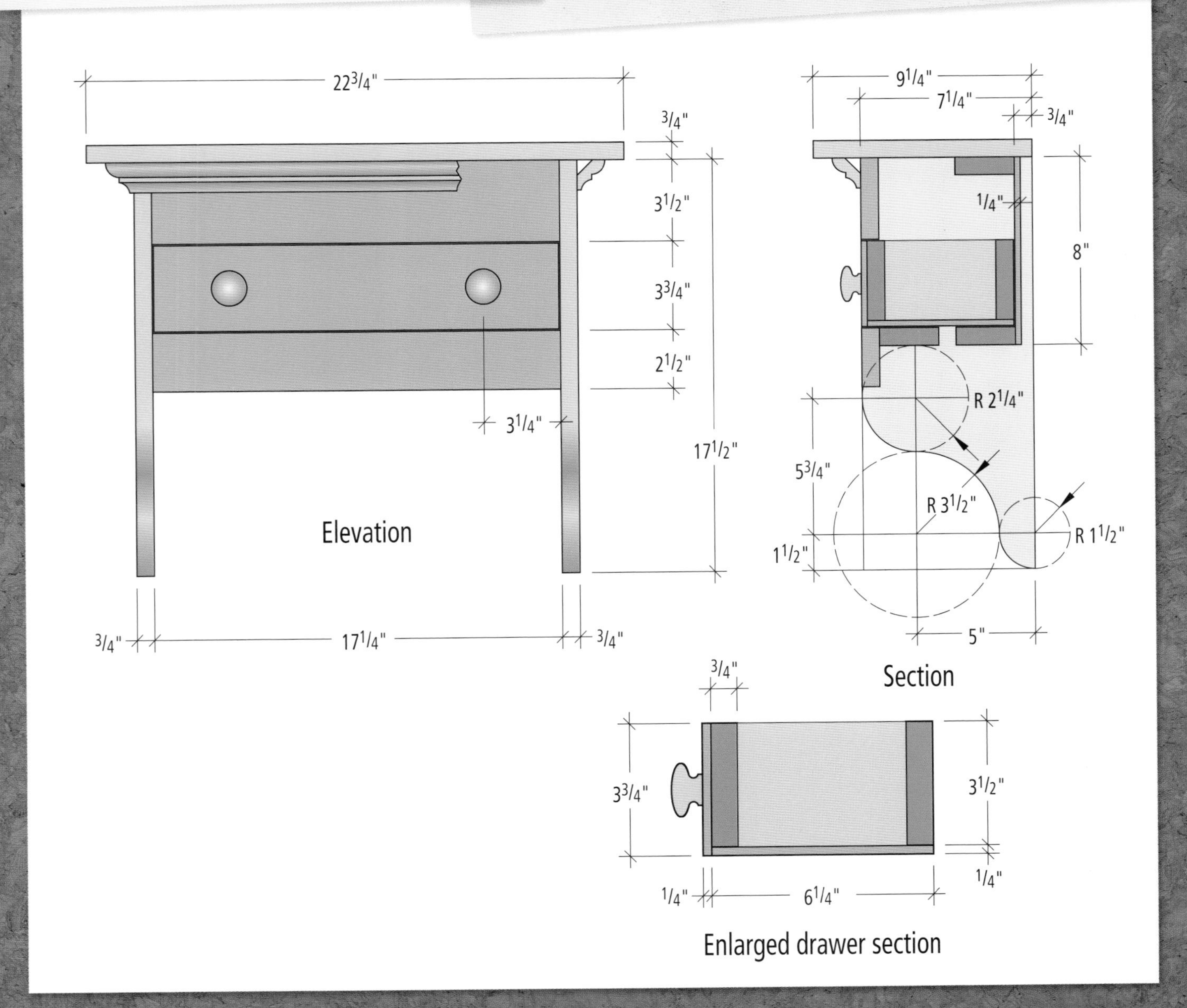

I've always felt that it seemed easier to cut a curved line with a jigsaw rather than a perfectly straight one. But don't get too comfortable when cutting these curves. Stay close to the line, but still on the waste side and take it slow so you'll have time to react if you cut too close.

Take a minute to mark out the location of all your pocket screws. Some of the rails will have four pockets, some will have more.

When drilling a pocket on the end of a tall piece, such as this side, make sure that the clamp is very secure and be conscious of the potential of the piece to rock side-to-side as you drill.

or scrap piece of 1/4" plywood. Either will give you a chance to get the shape perfect before transferring it to the actual piece of wood.

Cut the profile with the jigsaw then clean up any rough edges with a rasp and sandpaper. Since you have two sides with identical shapes, it makes sense to gang the two sides together as you clean up the edges. This allows you to make sure that both shapes will be identical, even after filing and sanding.

Next, square one end of the stock and crosscut the five rails that fit between the sides. Position and clamp a stop block at the miter saw to cut each piece to the same length. Then pull out the pocket-screw jig. You have holes to drill.

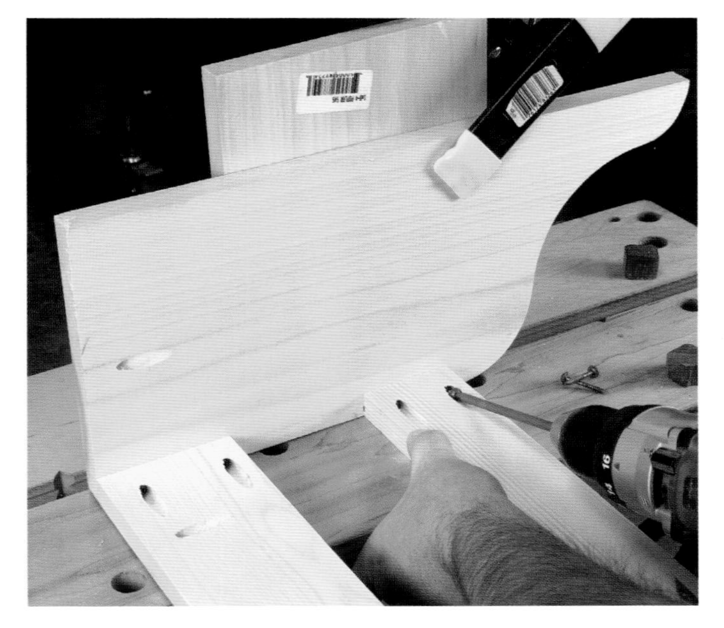

The first assembly step is to attach the top and lower face rails to the sides. Start with one side first, then spin the piece and attach the rails to the second side.

The partially assembled case is attached to the top. Make sure the case is centered from left to right on the top before putting in the screws. The nailing rail (not shown) is next attached to the sides.

The front drawer rail is next. It attaches to the sides and the front rail. A clamp makes it much easier to flush up the top edge of the front rail to the drawer rail as it's attached.

With the rear drawer rail in place, you're ready to attach the 1/4" back to the nailing rail and the rear drawer rail.

Each rail requires two pocket-screw holes per end. Also, the top face rail needs three extra holes, spaced evenly and along the grain, to attach the top. The drawer rail will need one hole that is centered, also along the grain, to hold the drawer rail flush with the lower face rail. It's a good idea to mark all of your boards before you start, to avoid any mistakes.

Step to Successful Assembly

The steps to assemble the case need to be completed in a specific order to allow you access to the pocket-screw holes. Follow the photos on this page to get the order right.

First, attach the top face rail and lower face rail flush with the front edge of the sides. Next, cut the top to length and position the partially assembled case on the underside of the top. Make sure the case is centered on the top and flush at the back edge. Add the screws and the top is attached.

Now attach the top nailing rail to the sides, holding it in 1/4" from the back edge of the sides . Then attach the front drawer rail to the lower face rail and the sides, followed by the rear drawer rail which is attached only to the two sides.

All that's left to assemble the case is to nail the back in place. Now for the crown.

The Crowning Moment

To fit the mouldings to the case, postion the project on its top with the front facing toward you as you work.

Set the miter saw at 45° to the right and position the moulding to the saw with the two flat areas on the back against the fence and table as shown above. Make the first cut leaving the side moulding extra long.

To make the second cut you need to swing the saw to 45° in the opposite direction, or to the left. Holding the moulding on the left side of the blade, make a cut that fully establishes the new angle on the stock.

Match those cuts to form the left-front corner. Hold the front moulding tight to the case and move to the right corner of the project and find the cut line.

Mark the cut line for the second cut on the front moulding as well as the angle of cut. Head back to the miter saw to complete the first cut for the right corner.

With the remainder of the stock you'll need to change the angle of the saw again and make a cut that mimics the second cut of the left corner. This gives you all the necessary pieces for your project.

Back at the project, position the first corner as before and add a 3d finish nail to the front moulding. Check the fit of the corners then complete the installation of the front moulding by driving nails into both the top and bottom of the profile as shown in the photo below left.

Position the side mouldings and mark a line at the back edge of the shelf (see photo below). The 90° cut is made with the moulding flat against the miter saw's table and tight to the fence.

Add glue to the miters for a bit of insurance to hold the miter joints tight, and attach the side mouldings with 3d nails too.

Use a nail set to set the heads of the nails just below the surface of the moulding — sometimes you can use a second nail for this step.

The best way to cut crown moulding at the miter saw is to position the moulding upside down to how it's installed on your project. As you mark the cut line, also note the direction of the 45° cut.

Marking the cut line for the second cut on moulding requires an exact layout. A ruler or straightedge held tight to the sides will reveal the location for the cut.

Two nails per corner, per piece will keep the corners tight. Pilot drilling for the nails will help avoid splits at the ends of your moulding.

After placing the return moulding tight against the corner miter, mark for the square cut, flush at the back of the case.

Building the drawer with pocket screws is a simple task. But, it is necessary to achieve a flush fit between the front and sides. The level joint makes the best connection when attaching the drawer face with glue.

Your jigsaw will do a decent job of cutting out the 1/4" plywood drawer face and drawer bottom, but a little clean up will be required. A block plane does a nice job on this thinner material.

Nails hold the bottom in place on the drawer. Center the nails carefully on the drawer sides or you might add an extra hole to the inside or outside of your drawer.

The aesthetics of the drawer, which shows no screws during normal use, is achieved by turning the pocket screws toward the outside of the drawer box and covering the front with the drawer face. Cut the face oversized and trim it flush with your plane.

Building an Inset Drawer

You already have the skills to build a drawer. You just need to know how to cut with a jigsaw, drill pocket-screw holes and hammer nails.

To properly fit an inset drawer, the front should be about 1/8" smaller than the opening — 1/16" on either edge. Measure the opening from side to side and subtract 1/8". Then subtract the thickness of the two sides (1 1/2") to arrive at the cut length of the front and back of the drawer box. Drill two pocket-screw holes at each end of the these pieces.

Next, cut the drawer sides to size and attach the front to the sides with pocket screws. Careful alignment of the joint makes attaching the drawer face easier. Complete the drawer box by installing the back piece.

The drawer bottom is 1/4" plywood. Measure the footprint of the box then cut the bottom with the jigsaw. Smooth rough cuts with a plane and attach the bottom with 3d nails.

Measure for the drawer face, including the thickness of the plywood bottom. Cut the plywood a little oversized, then add glue to the front rail of the drawer box, position the box onto the drawer face and add clamps as shown above.

Once the glue is dry trim the face with your plane, making the box and face flush on all sides. Finally, install store-bought wooden knobs.

To complete the shelf, knock off any sharp edges with 100-grit sandpaper, apply two coats of your favorite paint color, then cut and install the plywood back with 3d finish nails. Your Shaker-inspired shelf is ready to hang.

GAME TABLE

PROJECT 13

BY GLEN HUEY

Back in the day, gentlemen would sit for hours at the local barbershops and while away the time discussing the day's events and playing checkers. Hours might be spent sliding pieces from square to square.

Jumping the opponent's checkers was the way to clear his pieces from the board and to reach his back line where one would utter those fateful words, "king me". The king, two stacked checkers, possessed new powers that would allow it to move in new directions. With those added powers came a better chance at clearing the board.

Removing all of the opponents checkers would make one the winner. It would allow him to obtain the local title or possibly begin a heated argument that went on for days by itself.

What could be better than to bring those long passed days back into your home with the building of this game table? The time spent with family members playing at this table will bridge many gaps and start many a conversation about life.

It All Starts at the Top

The table top is the most important part of this table. That's where we begin. Select the material for the frame and make a 45° cut on both ends of the pieces leaving 23" of length at the long side of each piece. Cut all four pieces the same length.

The 23" figure comes about due to the size of the game board. The board is 18" square

PARTS LIST

			THICKNESS X WIDTH X LENGTH	
NO.	PART	STOCK	INCHES	MILLIMETERS
4	board frame	oak	$3/4 \times 2^1/2 \times 23$	19 × 64 × 584
4	board supports	poplar	$3/4 \times 1^1/2 \times 19^1/2$	19 × 38 × 495
1	board	plywood	$3/4 \times 18 \times 18$	19 × 457 × 457
2	inside fit aprons	poplar	$3/4 \times 3^1/2 \times 19^1/2$	19 × 89 × 495
2	outside fit aprons	poplar	$3/4 \times 3^1/2 \times 21$	19 × 89 × 533
4	legs (pre-miter)	poplar	$3/4 \times 3^1/2 \times 27$	19 × 89 × 686
2	leg connectors	poplar	$3/4 \times 2^1/2 \times 6$	19 × 64 × 152
2	stretchers	poplar	$3/4 \times 3^1/2 \times 19^1/2$	19 × 89 × 495

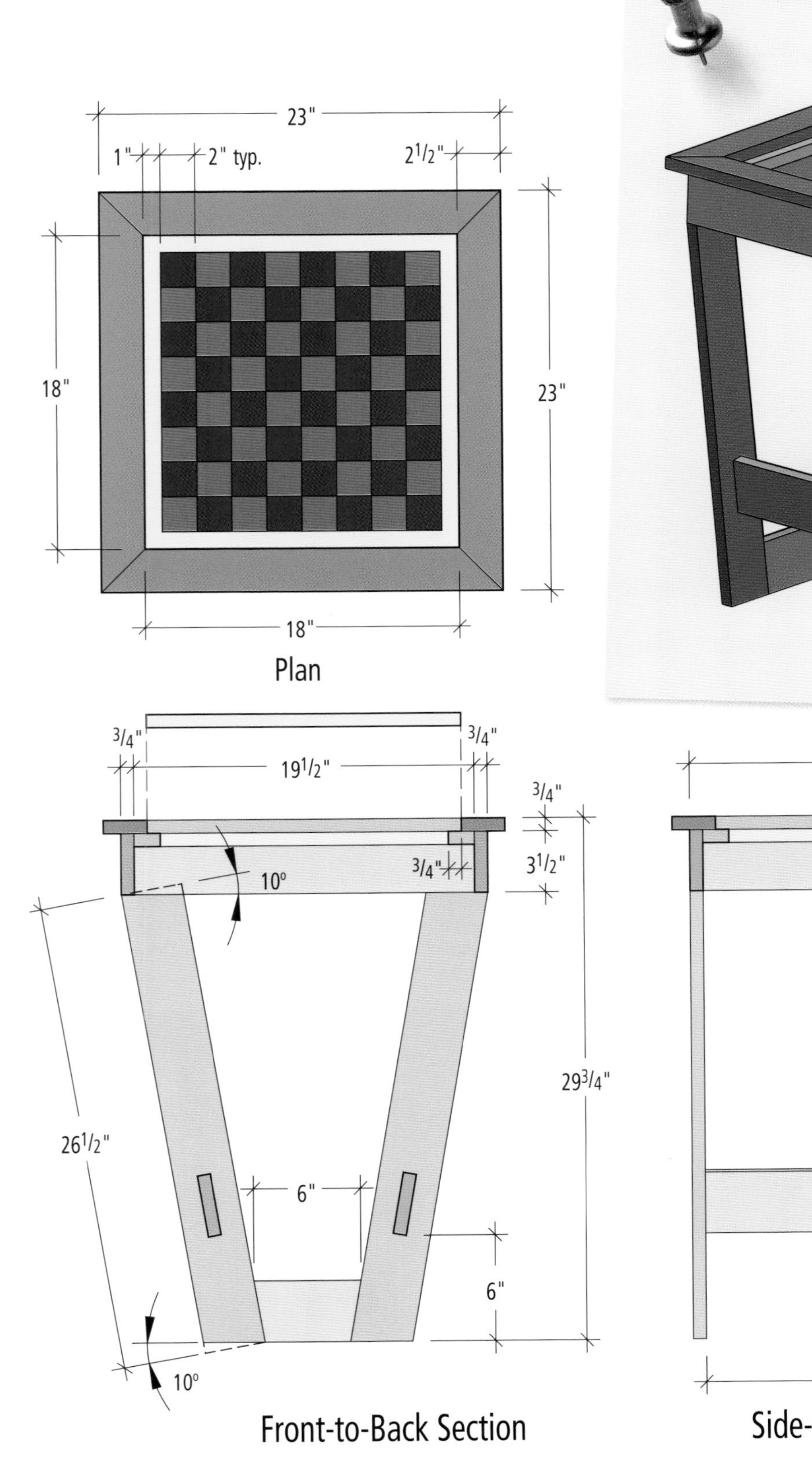

Front-to-Back Section

Side-to-Side Section

and using the stock for the frame at $2^1/_2$". To wrap the board with this stock you need to have pieces for the frame at 23". If you choose to change the board size remember to adjust the frame size as well.

With the frame pieces cut to length you'll need to use the pocket-screw jig to locate and drill two holes per end on two of the pieces (see photo below).

Putting the frame together is as simple as driving the pocket screws. Place a clamp on the piece that is accepting the screws so it won't move. Position the pocketed piece against the clamped frame member and drive the screws to make the connection. Repeat this step for each corner and the frame will come together.

For extra reinforcement I added screws to the corners (lower left) then cut plugs from matching stock to fill the countersink area. Any time during the project add a small amount of glue to the holes and tap in the plugs.

Next, prepare the stock for the board supports. Each piece has a mitered 45° cut at each end made at the miter saw. These pieces are attached to the inside edge of the frame with $^3/_4$" lying on the frame and $^3/_4$" sticking into the center area to catch the game board when it is positioned. Attach the support pieces with #8 x $1^1/_4$" wood screws. Be sure to use the tapered countersink for these holes too.

A Strong Leg to Stand On

The apron for the table is built to snugly fit around the support pieces. The best method to gather accurate sizes is to use the support frame to align the apron. Two pieces are the inside fit aprons. These pieces are cut to the same length as the support pieces. The two outside fit aprons will extend past the support pieces and cover the ends of the inside fit aprons. Return to the pocket-screw jig to cut two holes per end on the inside fit apron pieces.

With the holes cut connect the apron pieces with the pocket screws. The assembled apron should just slip over the support pieces and allow the top to fit into the apron. Don't make the connection of

Set the angled cut flat to the jig and drill the holes perpendicular to the cut end. The remaining pieces will accept the screws and no holes are required.

When driving the pocket screws, it's best to clamp whatever you can to the bench. This helps to ensure a tight, flush fit when the screw is tight.

Drill a hole with a tapered countersink at each corner, four in total, then add a screw to help to hold the corners of the frame tight.

Attach the board supports using screws.

Fit the apron parts to the board supports.

Use pocket-hole screws to assemble the apron parts.

Using a miter saw, cut a 10° miter on both ends of each leg. These cuts should be parallel.

After cutting the leg connectors to length, attach them to the legs. Make two of these leg assemblies.

the top to the apron just yet. You'll want to separate the two assemblies before you are finished with construction.

The legs are started at the miter saw. Set the saw for an 80° cut or 10° off of a square cut of 90°. Position the material for two legs at the saw and cut the angle at what is to be the top of each leg. Leave the saw set at that angle for the next set of cuts on the legs.

Set the top apron assembly on one side and position the angled cut on a leg against the bottom edge of the aprons. Pull a measuring tape from the bottom edge of the apron and mark at 25½" down the leg. This is where the second cut of the leg is placed.

Making that second cut is a snap. Position the leg material so that both legs are flush at the top end and cradled into the saw tight to the fence. Slide the two pieces, making sure that they stay aligned, into position to make another angled cut at the mark (lower left photo). It is important to have the cuts angled the correct way. When this cut is complete you'll have a parallelogram shape to the legs or both cuts angle in the same direction. Repeat the steps for the second set of legs.

Next, add pocket-screw holes to the top end of each leg and align them with the bottom edge of the apron making sure that the edge of the leg lines up with the side of the apron. It doesn't really matter which opposing aprons you select to attach the legs to since the apron is square, but I attached the legs so the end grain of the outside aprons sat on the leg top — there may be additional support with this choice.

Add the legs to one side of the table, then cut the leg connector to fit in position. This connector also cuts at the same angle as the legs. Make the cut on one end then flip the piece, measure the distance between the legs at a mark that is 2½" above the floor and make the second cut at that point. In this scenario you'll have the cuts set at opposing angles. Place two pocket-screw holes at each end and attach the connector to the legs. Repeat the

Attach each leg assembly to the bottom of the apron assembly using pocket screws.

Lay out the location for the stretchers and attach them to the legs.

process for the second leg assembly and you're ready for the stretchers.

The stretchers have square cut ends and pocket holes, two at each end, that allow you to attach them to the legs. Position the stretchers to the legs with the screw holes facing inside the table. I like these stretchers to be centered in the leg. To accomplish this easily I cut a scrap at the miter saw to the appropriate width, 1$^3/_8$" for this example, placed it at the front edge of the leg, pulled the stretchers tight to the back of the scrap and set the screws to make the connection. The base is complete.

Making the Game Board

Cut and fit the piece of plywood that is the game board to the opening in the table. This piece should be a loose fit so it can be removed if necessary. You see, you can also have a different game on the bottom of the board.

To mill this board use your jigsaw to cut close to the layout lines and then hand plane to bring everything into shape. Remember that if you're cutting across the grain of the plywood it is best to score a line with a sharp utility knife before cutting. That way as you cut to the line the top veneer of the plywood will not splinter.

Once the game board is fit you are ready to complete the table. Add the plugs to the top frame if you haven't already, install pocket-hole fillers into any hole that is easily visible and sand everything to 150 grit. Use 100-grit sandpaper to knock off any sharp edges and move to the finishing stage.

The game board is a checker board and to make your own board you need a few additional tools. Gather a utility knife, framing square (or square of some kind) and a roll of painter's tape that is 2" wide. Of course you'll need two or three different colors of acrylic latex paint.

To begin the board you'll need to layout the lines that define the checker squares. Find the center of the board and draw a line across the entire piece. Next, move each way in 2" increments each time, drawing a line as before. You should end up with eight squares and 1" of space on either edge which will be the outside border of the board.

Rotate the board 90° and repeat these steps for the opposing lines. Make sure that you continue the lines clear to the edge of the plywood piece. These will become important after the first layer of paint. You now have the sixty-four spaces for the checkerboard.

Paint Makes the Square

Add painter's tape to the outside edges of the squares which protects the borders from the first paint color. Traditionally, black and red are the colors of the checkerboard, but there is no reason you couldn't choose different colors. I selected black for the first layer. Whatever color you decide upon, make the first layer the darker of the two.

Apply the paint in a light coat moving from side to side on the board. When that coat is dry (you can speed it along with a hair dryer), add a second coat of the same color, brushing in the perpendicular direction. This coat completes the first layer of paint.

Remove the tape from the borders. See those lines for the layout? Stretch the tape from end to end aligning it with the lines. Apply tape to every other section as shown. Rotate the board and add tape in the second direction as well.

Now you need to remove the tape from any areas where the tape is double layered. Align the rule or straightedge to the tape and use a utility knife to cut the tape on all four sides of each square that needs to be removed. Carefully peel away the tape to expose the black painted surface below. Each square will be two thicknesses of tape.

Once the necessary areas are removed it is time to add paint. For this layer you need the second color and two coats will be needed to cover the exposed areas. Begin by brushing on one coat of paint moving from top to bottom. The second coat will be applied moving from side to side. This process provides better coverage. After the second layer is dry you can peel all remaining tape to expose the painted checkerboard.

Measure and mark the game board itself, using the table frame as your guide.

To lay out the checker grid itself, start from the center and measure out. It's much easier.

After taping off the 1" border, a base coat of black paint is applied to the whole board.

Tape is first stuck down in one direction, skipping every other space. This pattern is repeated in the other direction, then the tape is trimmed and removed where doubled.

Two coats of red paint are then applied over all the exposed squares. Again alternate directions between coats to hide brush strokes.

With the paint dry, the tape is removed, and the checkerboard pattern is revealed. I retaped the board to add a third contrasting color to the bare wood border.

To complete the painting you will need to apply tape around the outer edge of the checkerboard. The tape will be the barrier that will prohibit paint from touching the completed squares. I elected to paint a third color – one that will show favorably against the oak of the frame. You can also decide to allow the border to match the second color added to the checkerboard.

The completed board fits into the frame of the top. All that's left to complete the project is to apply paint to the base (I used black and added a layer of an oil/varnish finish for protection) and to apply two coats of Watco's Special Walnut finish to the oak.

Set this game table in your home and rekindle the past with a rousing game of checkers. Will you be kinged and become the local champion or have to succumb to another master of the house?

To complete the table I applied a couple of coats of black paint to the base, then added a top coat to protect the paint from scuffing. Finally, I added a coat of Watco oil to the top/frame of the table.

PATIO CHAIR

PROJECT 14

BY A.J. HAMLER

I've always envied bakers, working around that fresh-baked aroma all day. This cedar patio chair – the best-smelling project you'll ever make – will have you feeling the same way.

Cedar is straight-grained, with minimal shrinkage and expansion, and doesn't cup or twist as much as other softwoods. It works very easily, and it's the perfect wood for outdoor furniture as it naturally resists water, decay and insect damage.

Cedar comes in several species. Aromatic cedar, commonly used in hope chests and closet linings, smells great. But because the trees grow so slowly (a 20-year-old tree may be no more than 20' tall) it's on the expensive side for larger projects, plus it'll require a special order from a lumber company. Spanish cedar is less expensive, but the dust can be an irritant for many. And it's still a special order.

But Western red cedar – I'll just call it cedar from this point forward – is the perfect compromise. It's inexpensive enough for furniture, most people don't find it an irritant and, best of all, you can find at home centers. And then there's that aroma. Believe me, you'll be think-

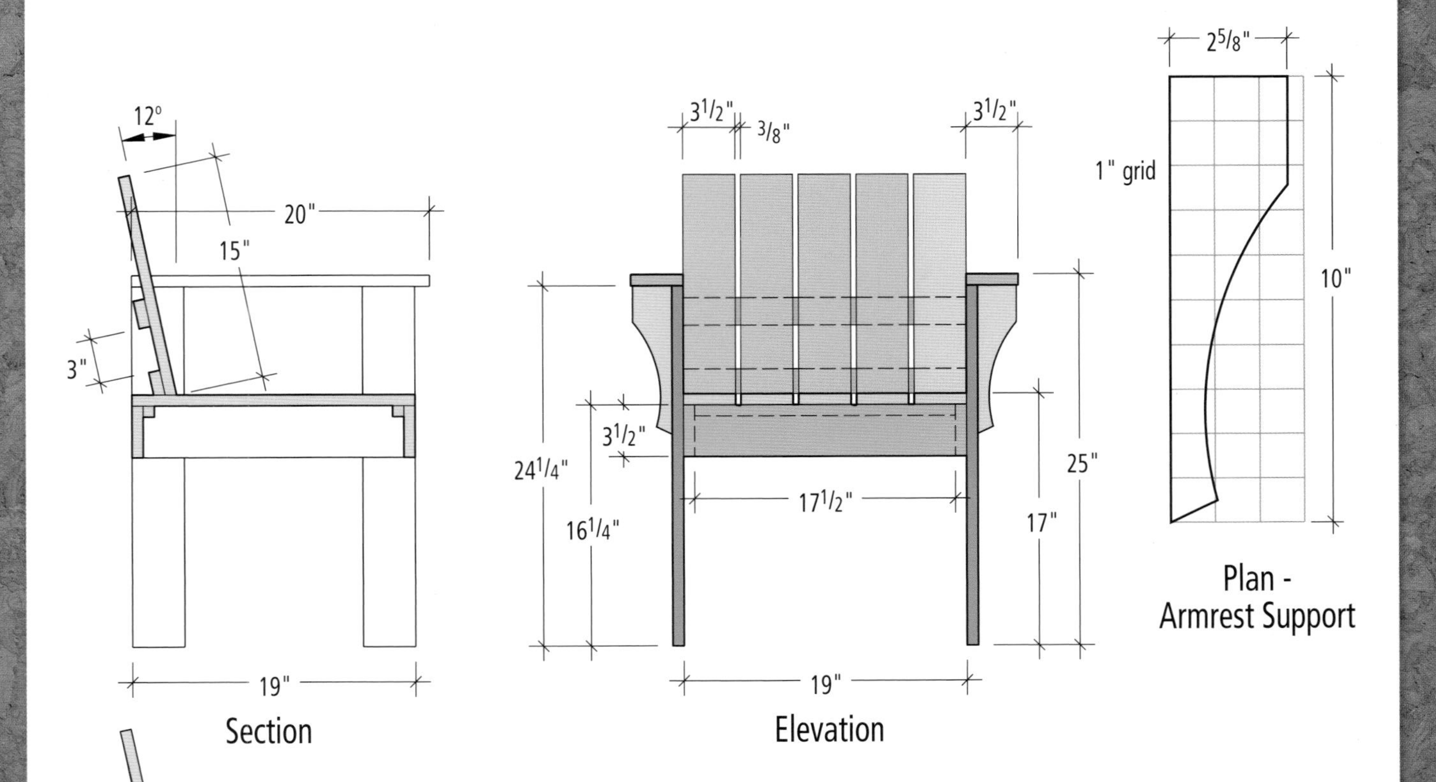

Section

Elevation

Plan -
Armrest Support

10"

Profile

PARTS LIST

			THICKNESS X WIDTH X LENGTH	
NO.	PART	STOCK	INCHES	MILLIMETERS
4	legs	cedar	$3/4 \times 3^1/2 \times 24^1/4$	19 × 89 × 616
4	armrest supports	cedar	$3/4 \times 2^5/8 \times 10$	19 × 67 × 254
2	armrests	cedar	$3/4 \times 3^1/2 \times 20$	19 × 89 × 508
2	seat box front/back	cedar	$3/4 \times 3^1/2 \times 19$	19 × 89 × 483
2	seat box sides	cedar	$3/4 \times 3^1/2 \times 17^1/2$	19 × 89 × 445
5	seat slats	cedar	$3/4 \times 3^1/2 \times 19$	19 × 89 × 483
2	slat support cleats	cedar	$3/4 \times 3/4 \times 17^1/2$	19 × 19 × 445
5	backrest slats	cedar	$3/4 \times 3^1/2 \times 15$	19 × 89 × 381
2	backrest braces	cedar	$3/4 \times 2 \times 19$	19 × 51 × 483

ing up excuses to make more cuts just to release another burst of that great smell into the shop.

Because this is an outdoor project, we'll use stainless steel screws wherever it may get wet. The stainless steel screws I bought are star drive. Star drive screws are fun to use, and the driver bit (included in the package with the screws) makes a very positive contact with the screw for sure driving; it'll even hold the screw without assistance. The pocket hole screws used for the seat box are protected underneath, as are the screws attaching the seat slats, so no need for stainless there. Speaking of waterproofing, if your finished chair will actually be out in the rain, consider using a waterproof glue such as Titebond III.

Almost all of the components for this chair measure $3/4$" × $3\,1/2$", the actual dimensions of a nominal 1 × 4, so everything can be made from 1 × 4 cedar right out of the rack. That means most of the cuts are crosscuts and you won't need to do much ripping. Buy enough stock to be able to cut your components to avoid knots. (Alternatively, you can save money by purchasing 1 × 8 boards and ripping up your own $3\,1/2$" stock. I've found that wider boards are generally more attractive and in better shape in the racks than narrower boards.)

Keep in mind that 1 × 4 dimensional stock can vary a bit – it may be slightly more or less than exactly $3\,1/2$" — so cut components accordingly. It's all right if the widths aren't quite the same, as long as you group like widths together. For example, if one board is slightly more than $3\,1/2$" wide, cut all the legs from that.

Also, cedar sometimes varies in thickness; some I bought was as much as $7/8$" thick. Again, this isn't a problem as long as you group like thicknesses together, and make minor alterations to project dimensions as needed. Another quirk of cedar boards is that one side is smooth while the other is almost always rough. No problem; just orient the boards with the rough side down or to the rear of the chair.

The stainless steel screws used for this project are self-drilling, and feature a star-drive head.

Mission Meets Mountain

The design of this chair blends the classic look of Mission style with the construction details and outdoor hardiness of Adirondack furniture. I retained the overall shape and arm/leg details of a Morris chair, joined with the slat appearance of an Adirondack chair. Overall, I think the effect works nicely. Little attempt is made to hide the screws in Adirondack chairs, but most are hidden in this chair, making for a smooth, unblemished appearance.

The project consists of three main sections: sides, seat and backrest. It doesn't

Since we're using standard 1 × 4 lumber, most of the cutting you'll do will be crosscutting, which can be quickly handled on the miter saw.

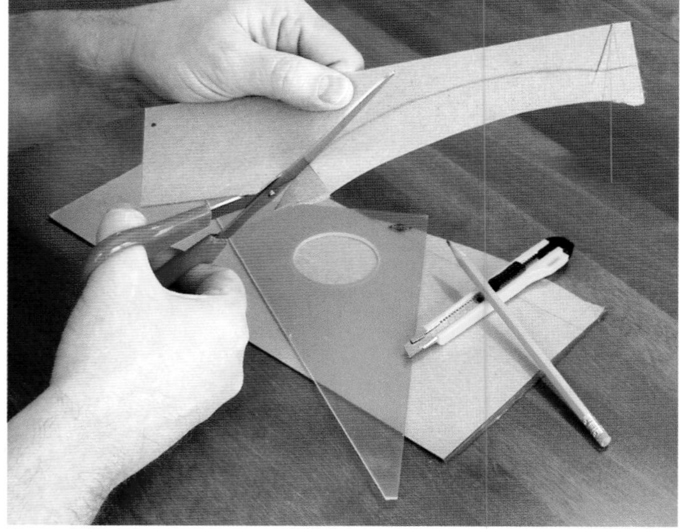
Transferring the pattern for the curved armrest supports to the workpieces is easier if you first cut a template out of stiff cardboard.

Cut out the armrest supports with a jigsaw. To keep the smooth sides facing forward on the finished chair, note how I've alternated the pattern to create *left* and *right* pieces.

Mark the tops of each leg as a guide to the exact center for attaching the armrest supports. Be sure to mark the legs *right* and *left* for proper orientation.

matter if you do the sides or the seat first, as long as you save the backrest for last to take exact measurements from the assembled chair for a perfect fit.

Start by cutting the legs and armrests to length on your miter saw. Set these aside for now.

Trace the outline for the curved armrest supports onto a piece of cardboard, and use this to transfer the pattern onto a workpiece at least 41" long.Cut out the four supports with a jigsaw. Mark a center line on the top end of each leg and align the supports, then glue and clamp them in place. Don't forget to mark the sets for *left* and *right*. Drill a pair of countersunk holes on the inside of each leg into the supports and attach securely with screws. I used a 2" screw at the top, and a 1¼" screw at the bottom. Locate the bottom screw so it will be hidden by the seat.

Attach the armrest by first gluing and clamping it to the leg pair for each side, making sure there is a 1" overhang at the front leg, then use a countersink bit to drill and then drive screws up through the back of the armrest supports and into the armrests from underneath.

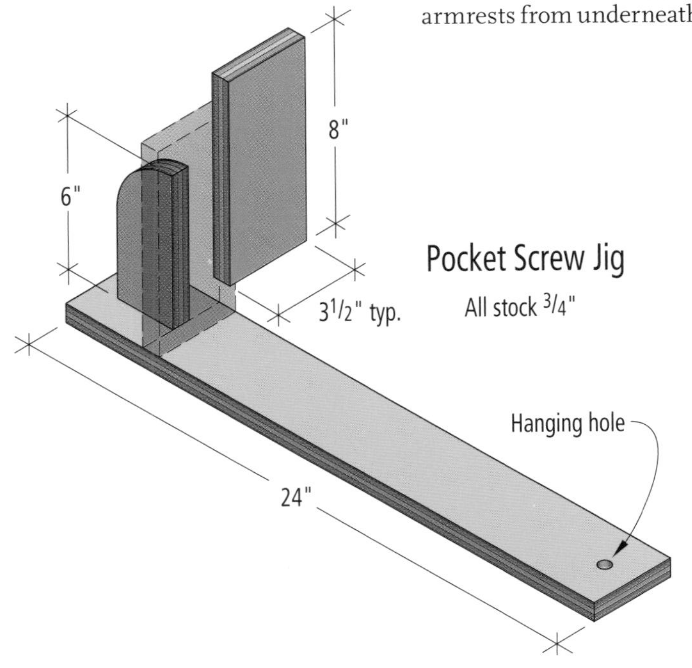

Take a Seat

The seat box is done as one unit, joined with pocket hole screws. Crosscut the seat box pieces to length and center the inside end of each of the side pieces in the pocket hole jig. Use the outer guides to drill a pair of holes using the ¾" setting. Note that I've attached my jig to a mounting board, which clamps securely to the workbench.

Assembling pocket hole joints in face frames using the jig's locking face clamp is simple, but joining boards end-to-end is more difficult, as the joints tend to move apart when driving screws in. I solved that by making a right-angle clamping fixture, into which I put both workpieces. Clamped securely at a 90-degree angle, the joint holds together perfectly when driving the screws. (By the way, I drilled a hole into the end of this assembly fixture and my pocket hole jig mounting board, so both can be hung on the shop wall when not in use.)

Basic Assembly

With the leg sets lying flat, mount the finished seat box to the inside surface with three countersunk 1¼" screws after gluing and clamping it into place. I attached the seat box so the top edge is 8¾" below the top surface of the armrests, but you can adjust this a bit if you like. A couple of pieces of scrap support the leg set to keep it level while working.

With the workpiece clamped securely in the jig, use the two outer guides to drill the holes for the washer-head pocket screws.

With the seat box and leg sets assembled, glue and screw a $\frac{3}{4}$" × $\frac{3}{4}$" cleat at the inside front and back, flush with the top of the seat box.

Crosscut the five seat slats to length and arrange them on the seat box — the two outside slats should be flush with the leg sets, but the interior slats should be spaced equally — and mark with a pencil. If your slats are a true $3\frac{1}{2}$", the spacing will be just over $\frac{1}{4}$". Adjust accordingly for your stock.

Attach the two outside slats first. Glue and clamp them in place, then upend the chair and drive a pair of countersunk $1\frac{1}{4}$" screws through the cleats and into each end of the slat. Repeat with the three interior slats, being careful to maintain equal spacing.

Cut a pair of $\frac{3}{4}$" × 2"back braces, measuring the inside width of the assembled chair to get the exact length for a perfect, snug fit between the leg sets. With the backrest slats crosscut to length, hold the lower backrest brace in place and mount the slats with glue and $1\frac{1}{4}$" screws countersunk through the brace from the rear. As before, start with the outside slats then add the interior slats one at a time, matching the spacing on the seat slats. Fasten the upper brace in the same way; the exact location of the upper brace isn't critical as

A shop-made right-angle clamping fixture keeps the drilled workpieces securely in place when driving the pocket screws

Attach the completed seat box to the leg sets with three countersunk $1\frac{1}{4}$" screws. Scrap wood under the leg set keeps everything level.

Countersink from the underside to drive screws to attach the seat slats. Since these screws are protected on the underside of the chair, I opted for regular screws here instead of stainless steel.

Although it isn't attached at this point, assembling the backrest inside the chair ensures a perfect, snug fit. Be sure the spacing of the backrest slats matches those in the seat.

With the jigsaw set at 12°, cut the bevel into the bottom edge of the backrest.

Drive a pair of 2" screws through each side of the leg sets to attach the backrest in place. The screws should anchor into the outside vertical slats, not the horizontal back braces.

long as it's below the rear of the armrest. Although not yet attached, the backrest should be a snug fit when finished.

Remove the assembled backrest from the chair to cut the bevel on the bottom. I opted for a 12° angle for the back, but you can adjust this a few degrees either way to your taste. Set your jigsaw to make the angled cut, and trim the bottom of the backrest through both the brace and slats, making doubly sure to cut the angle in the right direction. Touch up the angled edge with a sanding block if necessary.

Put the backrest in place on the chair and set the angle so the bottom bevel is flush with the seat slats. Countersink and drive two 2"screws through the leg sets into the sides of the backrest. Locate the screws so they anchor into the outside back slats, not the ends of the back braces.

Finishing Up

Sand all upper and outside surfaces, round over the front edges of the seat slats, and your patio chair is done. Because cedar is so hardy in outdoor environments, no protective finish is needed. The cedar will weather nicely on its own, gradually acquiring a darker patina.

Should you ever desire to return your chair to a like-new appearance, a simple resanding will make the cedar look fresh-cut. (And give you an excuse to fill your shop with that delightful aroma once again.

PRINTER STAND

PROJECT 15

BY DAVE GRIESMANN

We recently switched from a desktop computer, opting for a laptop for the convenience and portability. Since our laptop had wireless built in we decided that our computer desk was no longer necessary and got rid of it. While we were enjoying all our new-found freedom, we quickly realized that the computer still needed a home. Having our wireless router and printer on the floor was a less then desirable situation as well. So I set about to design and build an easy but functional printer stand that could also house our wireless router — and our laptop, when it was not in use.

I came up with the open-frame, three-level design you see here. It has the benefit of decent storage, but isn't an enclosed box, so it appears less massive. It also has a very small footprint, so It won't fill up the room. And, it has the benefit of being simple to build with just a few tools and a few hours.

I headed to the home center for my materials. I needed some 3/4" red oak boards, and four 2 × 2 × 36" pieces to use for my legs. I thought about using thinner material for the legs, but I liked the look and support that these beefier pieces allowed.

What's Your Angle?

Starting with two of my 2 × 2 pieces I made a 90° cut at the ends to assure a square end. I wanted the upper part of my legs to tilt towards the back of the stand by 30°. In order to make the thickness of the legs match at the joint I needed to cut both sections at a 15° angle so that when joined, the angle would provide my 30° tilt.

Squaring over one end of a stock piece of material is important, especially if it's going to be a table or chair. If your ends aren't flat, the piece of furniture will wobble once in place.

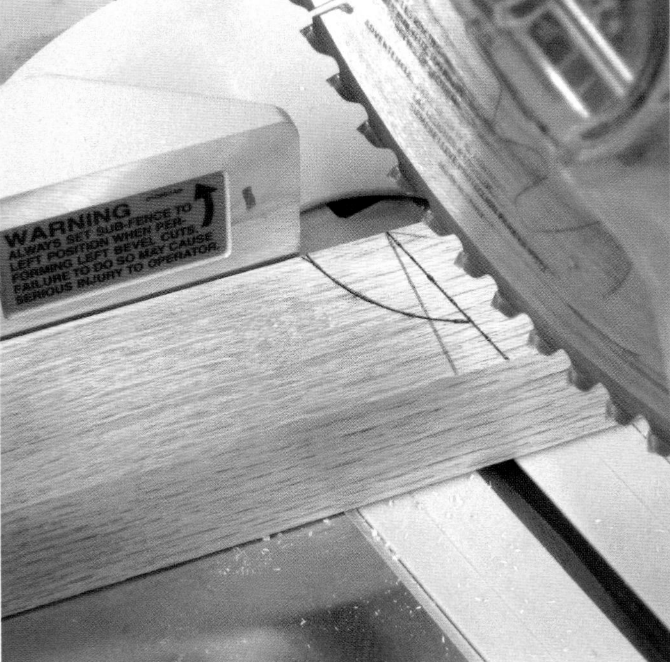

After squaring one end of the leg on the miter saw, I marked my 15° angle at the appropriate point on the leg, adjusted the saw and made my cut.

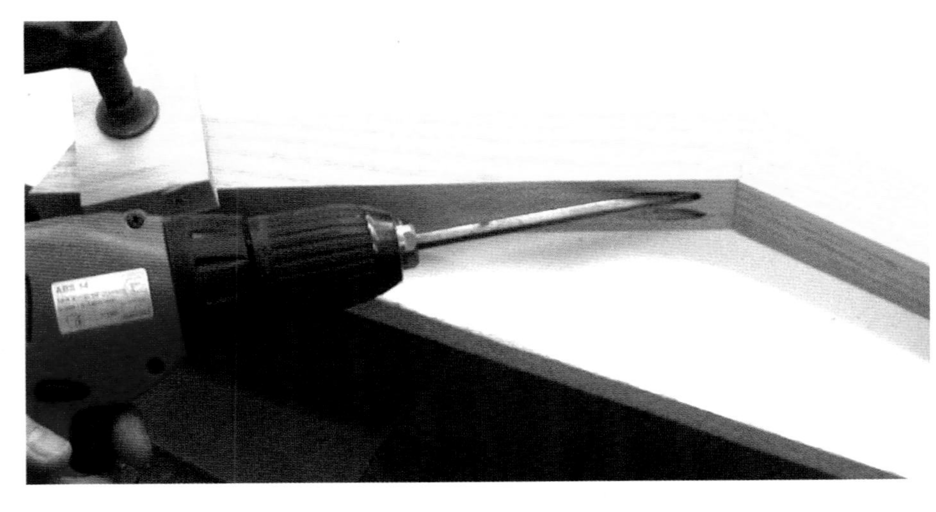

To assemble this unusual angled joint, normal clamps just didn't work. Instead I clamped the two leg pieces in position on a flat surface and then went ahead and assembled the joint.

I measured up $24\frac{7}{16}$" from the squared ends and marked a 15° cut on the outside edge of the leg, angling the cut toward the inside of the leg. I made the cut on both those pieces, then moved to the top part of the legs.

I flipped the fall-off from my first cuts around and with the saw still set to 15°, I again made two cuts. To cut the top part of the legs to length I measuree $11\frac{7}{8}$" from the longest point to longest point and set my saw to cut a 60° angle on the opposite end. Make sure you're making the cut in the proper direction. For the back legs I squared up one end of each and then measured up 34" and cut another 90° angle.

Knee Joint

Using my pocket screw jig I cut two pocket screw slots into the inside of the top pieces of the front legs (the least visible location for the screw pockets). With this complete I use a couple of clamps and some glue to hold the two parts of the leg together and then pocket screw each leg together.

Each of the side stretcher pieces get two pocket holes per end to attach them to the leg pieces. The same goes for the front and rear stretchers for a total of eight stretcher pieces.

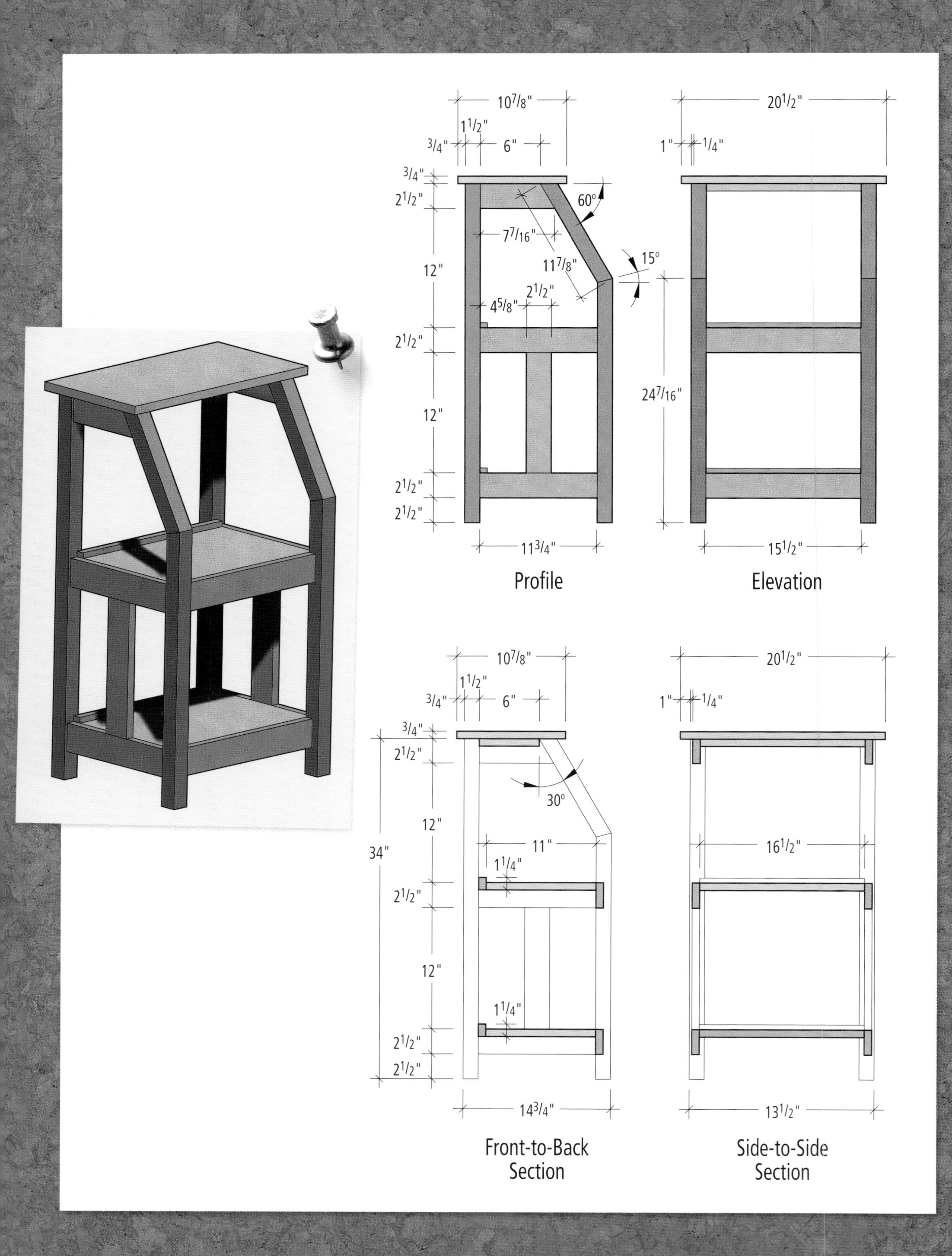
10 7/8"
1 1/2"
3/4"
6"
3/4"
2 1/2"
60°
7 7/16"
15°
12"
11 7/8"
2 1/2"
4 5/8"
2 1/2"
12"
2 1/2"
2 1/2"
11 3/4"
Profile
20 1/2"
1"
1/4"
24 7/16"
15 1/2"
Elevation
10 7/8"
1 1/2"
3/4"
6"
3/4"
2 1/2"
30°
12"
34"
11"
1 1/4"
2 1/2"
12"
1 1/4"
2 1/2"
2 1/2"
14 3/4"
Front-to-Back
Section
20 1/2"
1"
1/4"
16 1/2"
13 1/2"
Side-to-Side
Section

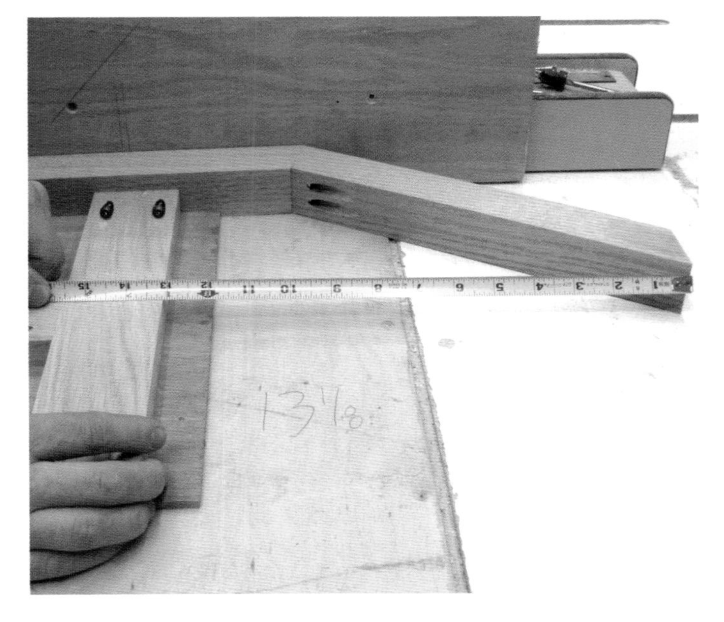

To determine the location of the side stretcher assembly, I measured down 13" from the top of the leg. This is actually easier to do with the side assembly, so you don't have to transfer the location.

Rather than have the stretchers flush to the outside of the legs, I used a piece of 1/8" plywood to raise the side assembly as I attached it to the legs, giving a simple offset, without having to measure.

Lots of Stretchers

With this completed I now turn my attention to the side and front stretchers. Using my miter saw, I square up the ends of four long pieces. Then I measure and cut four pieces at 11 3/4" for the side stretchers, four more pieces at 15 1/2" for the front stretchers and two more pieces at 12" for the middle risers for the side assembly.

With these eight pieces cut to size I drill four pocket hole slots into each piece. Setting the front stretchers aside I mark the middle of the side stretchers and pocket screw a riser to them to form an *I* for each side assembly.

To give the piece a shadow line, I lay the sides face down and use a scrap piece of 1/8" plywood as a spacer and lay my *I* assembly on top of it. Measuring down 13" from the top of the leg, I determine the location of the top of the stretcher assembly and then attach it to both the front and back legs with pocket screws.

The top stretchers on the two sides need to fit inside the angle formed by the front leg. To figure out that angle I use the side itself rather than trying to measure. I first cut a 90° angle on one end of the stretcher and then lay the piece underneath the front leg to mark the exact angle of the cut. I then headed back to my miter saw and set the saw to match my pieces, then made the cuts.

With the two top stretchers cut to size I turn back to my pocket hole jig to cut four slots in each piece. This step is a little tricky, so get your thinking cap on. Two of the slots (on the angled end of the stretcher) need to be cut in line with the angled end to assure maximum holding power to the leg. Again utilizing my 1/8" plywood as a spacer I attach my top stretchers to the legs.

PARTS LIST

NO.	PART	STOCK	THICKNESS X WIDTH X LENGTH INCHES	MILLIMETERS
1	top	oak	3/4 x 10 7/8 x 20 1/2	19 x 276 x 521
1	sub top	oak	3/4 x 6 x 15 1/2	19 x 152 x 394
2	shelves	oak	3/4 x 11 x 16 1/2	19 x 279 x 419
2	shelf lips	oak	3/4 x 1 1/4 x 16 1/2	19 x 32 x 419
2	stiles side top	oak	3/4 x 2 1/2 x 7 7/16	19 x 64 x 189
4	stiles side middle/bottom	oak	3/4 x 2 1/2 x 11 3/4	19 x 64 x 298
2	stiles front	oak	3/4 x 2 1/2 x 15 1/2	19 x 64 x 394
2	rails side	oak	3/4 x 2 1/2 x 12	19 x 64 x 305
2	legs back	oak	1 1/2 x 1 1/2 x 34	38 x 38 x 864
2	legs front	oak	1 1/2 x 1 1/2 x 35 7/16	38 x 38 x 900

Shelves Before Assembly

It's easier to add the two shelves and subtop before we add the last stretchers. My shelves are solid oak (and I had to do some edge gluing to get them to the proper width) but you could substitute plywood in your version. The edges of the shelves are all conveniently hidden by the stretchers and the back lips, so only you would know the diference.

I used my miter saw to cut my two shelves to 16 1/4" in length. If you have a sliding miter saw this cut is pretty simple, but since the shelf is 11"-wide a standard

Rather than trying to measure the angle for the end of the top stretcher, it's easier to just transfer the angle and location directly from the piece itself.

The pocket screws for the top side stretchers need to be perpendicular to the angle of the end. I used an extra piece of stretcher material to extend the width of the leg so that the pocket jig would be properly supported while cutting the angled end. Drilling the square end (shown) is once again a simple task.

You can increase the cutting width capacity of your circular saw by making the cut part way through the board, then flipping the piece to complete the cut. Just make sure you align your second cut carefully to avoid a stepped edge.

miter saw can't make that width of cut. Not in one pass, at least. You can still complete this cut by marking your line and cut as much as you can with one cut, then turn the board over and cut the other half of the cut. Simple.

Once you have the two shelves cut to size use your pocket-hole jig to drill three slots on each end. But before attaching the shelves, cut two pieces to of lumber to 3⁄4" × 1 1⁄4" × 16 1⁄4" to serve as back lips on your shelves. Glue these in place on the back edge. I also used few small brad nails to hold it in place while the glue dries.

While this dries I cut a piece of lumber to 3⁄4" × 6" × 16 1⁄4" for the sub-top. With this cut to size I drill three pocket-hole slots in each end.

With the three horizontal pieces cut to size (sub-top and two shelves) its time for some assembly. The two shelves are aligned to be flush with the top edge of the side stretchers. The sub-top is flush with the top edge of the top stretchers.

From here I attach my two front stretchers using pocket screws, glue and brad nails. Now it's time to start plugging the pocket hole slots that can be easily seen. The plugs were included with the pocket hole kit that my home center sold. Once you glue the plugs in and the glue dries you can sand the plugs flush. I put wood putty in the brad nail holes at the same time.

With the two shelves and the sub-top cut to size, the back lips attached to the shelves, and all the pocket holes drilled, you're ready to assemble. Start with one frame flat on your bench and attach the shelves, then flip the piece over onto the second side (laying flat on your bench) and finish the assembly. All that's left is the front rails and the top and you're done.

While everything was drying, I milled the top to $3/4" \times 10 7/8" \times 20 1/2"$ in size. I layed the top finished side down on my bench, then centered the frame upside down on the top. A few screws through the sub-top attached the top quickly.

Now I start final sanding the piece to 120 grit making sure to round all the sharp edges. Once this is complete I take a dripping wet towel and wipe the piece down with water. This will raise the grain and once the piece is dry I sand it again using 120-grit sandpaper.

Once the sanding is complete I apply two coats of clear wipe on poly and let it dry. For my last coat I wipe on a coat of Watco Danish Oil. This gives the oak a darker look.

I don't know why I couldn't find a stand like this in the store. It's the perfect size. But then it was a fun project, so why complain?

A simple coat or two of Danish Oil will give the oak color, character and protection.

PAINTED CUPBOARD

PROJECT 16

BY GLEN HUEY

Small cupboards fit anywhere in your home. This piece can hang in the kitchen to catch any pantry overflow or it can look equally impressive hanging in your living room showcasing your collectibles. Hey, you may even want to build two when you see how easy this cupboard is built.

This project will also serve as an excellent teaching tool for a dramatic finish. Once I walk you through the basic steps, you'll not only find out how much fun it can be to beat-up a finish (I'm not kidding), but you'll definitely say, "I can do that!"

Start by selecting and cutting to length the material for your shelves and the cupboard sides. The shelves will need to be ripped from the purchased stock. Draw a line on each piece that is 4¾" from one edge and make the cut along that line with the jigsaw.

If you're like most of us the cuts will need to be straightened up with your hand plane. Make sure that you keep the edge squared to the face of the piece and trimmed to the layout line.

Next, pull out your pocket-screw jig and place two holes at each end of the shelves. Since these will be inside the cupboard there is little need to select the top or bottom of each piece, however, you should study the case sides in order to place the best face toward the outside of the piece.

The Box is Formed

The building of the box begins with attaching the top and bottom shelves to the case sides. Make sure to align the front edges and install the pieces with the holes facing outward.

Most of the construction on this piece is done with pocket screws. This mini-pocket guide makes the work easy, allows you to work in tight spaces, and best of all, it's affordable!

Next, lay out the location of the middle shelf and attach it as well. You'll find it easier to drive the screws for the shelf if you cut a scrap to fit between the top shelf and the middle shelf. With pieces positioned as shown in the photo below, it would be impossible for the shelf to move as the screws are installed.

Flip the assembled portion of the case and install the second case side the same way. The only tricky spot might be adding the screws to the middle shelf because your drill may not fit in the open space.

Select and cut the case front stiles from your stock, position the box on its back and attach the pieces so that the edges of the stiles are flush to the sides of the box. Add a thin bead of glue for reinforcement and make the connection with flat-head woodscrews that are driven into holes made with a 3⁄8" countersink. You'll want to fill those holes with a matching 3⁄8" plug, then sand the assembly with #150-grit sandpaper.

Build the Flat Panel Door

The door is made from bead board tongue-and-groove panelling, but I found it in the home center stores referred to as reverse flooring. Call it what you want, it makes an easy frame for a frame-and-panel door. First you need to rip the tongue portion from three 24" pieces. Use the same process for this operation as you did to rip the shelves to width. Draw in the cut line, cut close with the jigsaw and clean up the cut with the hand plane.

Next, take the measurements for the four pieces that will make up the door's frame. Measure from top to bottom and subtract 1⁄8" to arrive at the length of the stiles. To get the length of the rails repeat the same step beginning with the width of the door opening.

There are two stiles and two rails. Off to the miter saw to make 45° cuts on both

When assembling the case, it's always smart to work down towards the bench, rather than trying to balance the sides on top of the shelves. Note the spacer I'm using to keep the shelves aligned accurately.

Rather than juggle the pieces to keep things flush, put a clamp across the piece and save the frustration.

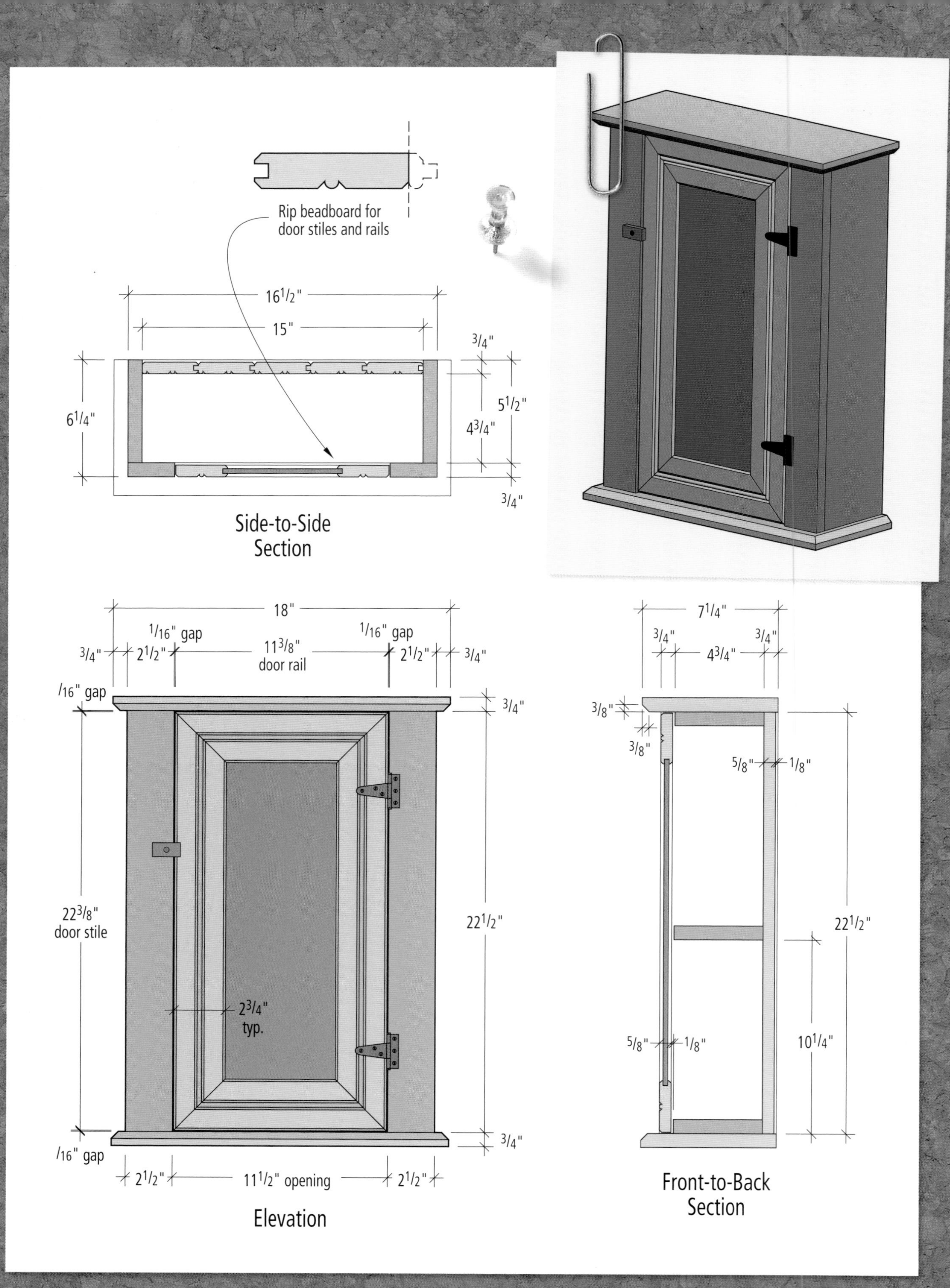

Rip beadboard for door stiles and rails
16 1/2"
15"
3/4"
5 1/2"
6 1/4"
4 3/4"
3/4"
Side-to-Side Section
18"
1/16" gap
1/16" gap
3/4"
2 1/2"
11 3/8" door rail
2 1/2"
3/4"
/16" gap
3/4"
22 3/8" door stile
22 1/2"
2 3/4" typ.
/16" gap
3/4"
2 1/2"
11 1/2" opening
2 1/2"
Elevation
7 1/4"
3/4"
3/4"
4 3/4"
3/8"
3/8"
5/8"
1/8"
22 1/2"
10 1/4"
5/8"
1/8"
Front-to-Back Section

The case front stiles define the space that the door will fit within. Hold the pieces flush to the case sides and fit the door to the space, rather than trying to allow the space for the door and trim the stiles. It's just easier. Countersunk flat head screws hold the stiles in place, and a little putty and sanding make them invisible once the piece is painted.

I'm particularly proud of using bead board material to create the door frame, though it does require a little extra ripping.

ends of all pieces. Cut the angles so that the groove is on the inside after the angles are added. You'll need that groove to hold the plywood panel. Either set up a stop block to ensure that the two stiles match in length as do the rails or, align the rails and cut both pieces at the same time. Repeat this step for the two stiles as well. Once cut, arrange the pieces to check the fit.

To make the connection of the angled pieces you are again going to use the pocket screw. Add the pocket-screw holes to the stiles of the door only and position the pocket-screw jig so that the pocket does not show from the edge of the door (next page bottom left photo). Prepare two pocket holes per corner of the door.

Driving the screws for the doorframe can be fussy. Position the pieces face down on your bench and add a clamp to the piece accepting the screws (next page top photo). Hold the matching piece in position and carefully drive the screws home. The accurate cutting of the angles

PARTS LIST

NO.	PART	STOCK	THICKNESS X WIDTH X LENGTH INCHES	MILLIMETERS
2	case sides	paint grade	$3/4 \times 5^1/2 \times 22^1/2$	19 × 140 × 572
2	case top and bottom	paint grade	$3/4 \times 7^1/4 \times 18$	19 × 184 × 457
2	case front sides	paint grade	$3/4 \times 2^1/2 \times 22^1/2$	19 × 64 × 572
3	shelves	paint grade	$3/4 \times 4^3/4 \times 15$	19 × 121 × 381
2	door rails	flooring	$5/8 \times 2^3/4 \times 11^1/2$	16 × 70 × 292
2	door stiles	flooring	$5/8 \times 2^3/4 \times 22^1/2$	16 × 70 × 572
1	flat panel	plywood	$1/4 \times 6^1/4 \times 17^1/4$	6 × 159 × 438
1	turn button	paint grade	$3/4 \times 1^1/2 \times 3/8$	19 × 38 × 10
-	back boards	flooring	$5/8 \times 14^7/8 \times 22^1/2$	16 × 378 × 572

One trick with the frame is making sure that all of your cuts leave the bead detail on the frame matching at the corners. It doesn't take much to kick the pattern out of whack.

will bring the frame into square as you attach the final corner.

With the frame assembled, take the measurement for the plywood or flat panel. You need to get accurate measurements then add 1/4" to the overall sizes to both the length and width. Cut the panel to size with the jigsaw and clean any cut marks with the plane. In crosscutting the plywood, if you score the line with a utility knife, you can reduce possible splintering and obtain a cleaner cut.

Remove all screws from one stile to allow the panel to slide into the frame. After the panel is installed, add the screws back to the frame and your door is built.

To hold the door frame together, I'm once again using pocket screws. The pockets need to be oriented across the corner joint, but drilled so that the pocket isn't visible from the edge of the door frame. Both the pieces in this picture are stiles. Don't cut any pockets in the rails, or you'll have twice as many holes as you need.

Clamping the door rail to your bench during assembly makes things easier to handle. Nothing like an extra hand to help.

Adding the Crowning Touch

The case is topped (and bottomed) with a separate piece of stock. Cut both pieces to size according to the cut sheet. In order to dress up the cupboard a bit, add a beveled edge to three sides of these pieces.

Draw a line on the ends and the front of both the top and bottom that is half the thickness of the stock or 3/8". Next, draw a line that is 3/8" in front the edges on those same three sides. A hand plane will remove the material between the two lines, creating the bevel.

Position the box onto the top and align the back edges. Slide the box along the top until the overhang is equal on both ends. Once set add screws through the box into the top. It's best to prepare these holes with a countersink bit. Repeat the steps to attach the bottom, also using four screws, one at each corner area. Clamps will keep everything held tight during this operation.

Don't forget to slip the panel into the frame before attaching the last stile.

The back boards for the cupboard are the same material that is used for the door frame. Take the measurements for the pieces and cut them to length. It is necessary to fit the first four pieces, position them into the case and find the correct width for the final piece of the back then reduce the measurement by 1⁄8". This will help with seasonal adjustments of the back due to humidity changes. It will need to be ripped to the final size.

Mark the exact width of the final piece beginning from the existing grooved edge of the stock. You'll cut the tongue area to complete the fit. Use the jigsaw to make the cut and straighten the cut with your hand plane. Remember this is the back and it fits tight to the sides as viewed from the interior of the case.

After finishing, nails are driven through the boards and into the shelves to install the back.

A simple champfer on the front and both side edges of the top and bottom pieces adds a simple, but effective detail to the finished look. Mark the defining edges of the champfer in pencil on the pieces and then use your block plane to remove the material. It sounds a little tedious, but it'as actually fun to add a hand-crafted detail to your piece.

The case is centered on both the top and bottom pieces, and they are attached using flat head screws in countersunk holes.

The first four pieces of the back remain full-width, and only the last piece is trimmed in width to fit the case.

The Stain, Paint, Rub Finish

The finishing process for the cupboard starts with staining the piece. Use an aniline dye stain that is mixed to the manufacturer's directions. It doesn't really matter what the exact color is, so long as it is a shade of brown.

Applying the stain could not be easier. Paint the stain onto the cupboard with a foam brush. Make sure that the entire piece is coated, with stain dripping from the wood. Allow that to sit for five minutes then wipe any excess away with a dry cloth.

Once the stain is dry, in about 6 -8 hours, lightly sand the cupboard with a 400-grit paper to knock down any raised grain (water will raise the grain of wood).

The next step is to add a coat of shellac. The best way to do this is with an aerosol can of shellac. With the can about six inches from the piece, add a single coat of sprayed shellac. The idea is to apply a level coat without any runs or drips, so keep the can moving. When you stop without stopping the spray, you will get runs. When the shellac is dry lightly sand the surface with 400-grit sandpaper.

Choose a paint color for the inside of the piece and paint the interior with two coats. Use an acrylic latex paint and don't forget the backboards. I like to select a color that is bold and will almost shock when the door is opened. The color should bounce off of the mellow painted exterior. Of course, you can pick and choose which colors you like best. The paint process is the same with each color.

Next, apply the paint to the exterior of the cupboard. Use an acrylic latex paint—I chose an off white, almost crème color. Work with small areas at a time because if the paint dries too quickly you won't be able to add the wear to the piece.

As the paint dries it will reach a point where it is dry enough to allow manipulation of the paint without smearing the surface. This is when you spring into action. Rub areas that will simulate ages of wear. Work around the turn button—this is where the greatest amount of wear would be in an antique piece. Create wear at the corners, along the top and bottom of the cupboard and lightly on the sides of the piece.

Apply the stain liberally using a foam brush. Let the stain penetrate the wood for about 5 minutes, then wipe off the excess using a dry cloth.

After the stain is dry, apply a coat of shellac. Keep the can moving while you're spraying to prevent the shellac from running or dripping.

Apply the paint with a foam brush. Let the paint dry for a few minutes, then begin rubbing the paint off in some areas. This will create wear areas and give the piece an old, used look.

Create as much wear as you like, but don't overdo it. It's easy to pass the antique look and get into the beaten up stage. The great thing about this process is that you can always go back and add paint to cover overly worn areas without it being obvious in the finished piece.

With the paint complete and dry add a coat of paste wax to the cupboard then install the hinges. I've darkened the regular strap style hinges from the home center with gun bluing that is used to color the steel on gun barrels.

Place the hinges and screws into the solution until they're black, remove them and allow all to dry. Always use rubber gloves and avoid letting the bluing mixture touch your skin.

The turn button is made from scrap. Begin with a 1½" wide portion chopped from one of the leftover pieces. Next spin the cut off at the miter saw and slice away the ⅜" thick piece that is the button. Smooth any sharp edges and add the screw into the center of the button. The turn button mounts ⅔ up the edge of the door on the case stile where it can spin to lock the door.

Add the backboards by nailing them with 4d finish nails, one nail per piece, located just off of the grooved edge, and the cupboard is ready for placement in your home.

Gun bluing will turn off-the-shelf hinges black, giving them the look of iron.

SIMPLE SIDE CHAIR

PROJECT 17

BY GLEN HUEY

After years of building furniture, mostly case pieces, I've come to understand that chair building is different. Where most casework involves working with panels and straight lumber, most chair building turns to bending stock or forming parts. When you find a chair that fits into the casework criteria, you should take every opportunity to build that piece.

This chair fits into that framework. I envision this chair sitting anywhere from around the dining room table, to welcoming guests to your home in the foyer, to being perched beside the dressing table in your bedroom. It is sturdy, comfortable and the construction is beginner friendly to say the least.

The focus of most chairs is the back and the seat. This chair has gathered the eye appeal with the shapely hour-glass back splat and the colorful seat that is woven with Shaker tape. One chair just might not be enough.

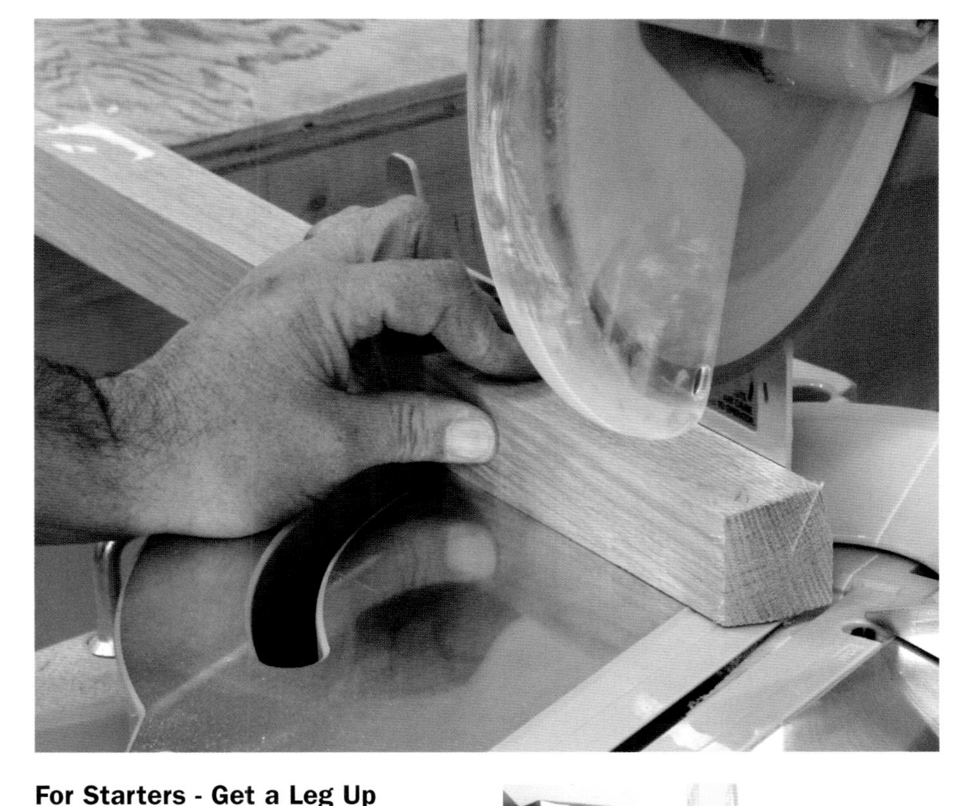

Set the miter saw to a five degree angle. Place the leg on the saw so that the cut begins about 1/2" down from the top of the leg. Use a stop block to hold the leg in place as you rotate the leg 90° to make the four cuts for each leg.

For Starters - Get a Leg Up

Building chairs begins with the legs. Since you've already got the width and thickness of the pieces (1 1/2" square) by buying stock material from the home center store, the next step is to cut them to length. You'll need two front legs that are 18" in length and two back legs that begin at 36" long.

To add interest to the chair, cut the top of each leg to a pyramid design. Set the miter saw to a 5° angle. Place the leg on the saw so that the cut begins about 1/2" down from the top of the leg. Four cuts are needed to create the pyramid – one at each face. Making the cuts is easy enough, but what might present a problem is aligning each cut to the previous cut.

This is best accomplished by setting a stop block to position each leg and each cut against. Place the leg against the block and make the first cut. Next, rotate the leg one turn and make the second cut. Repeat this pattern for each face and each leg. There is one set-up for the front legs and another for the back legs. The finished tops appear as small pyramids when viewed.

If you can't easily add a stop to your miter saw, you can also mark a line all the way around the top of each leg, 1/2" down from the top. This will be your cut line.

A chair is not comfortable if the back

The rear leg (left) needs only a slight (5°) angle cut on the bottom to add about fifty percent more comfort to your chair.

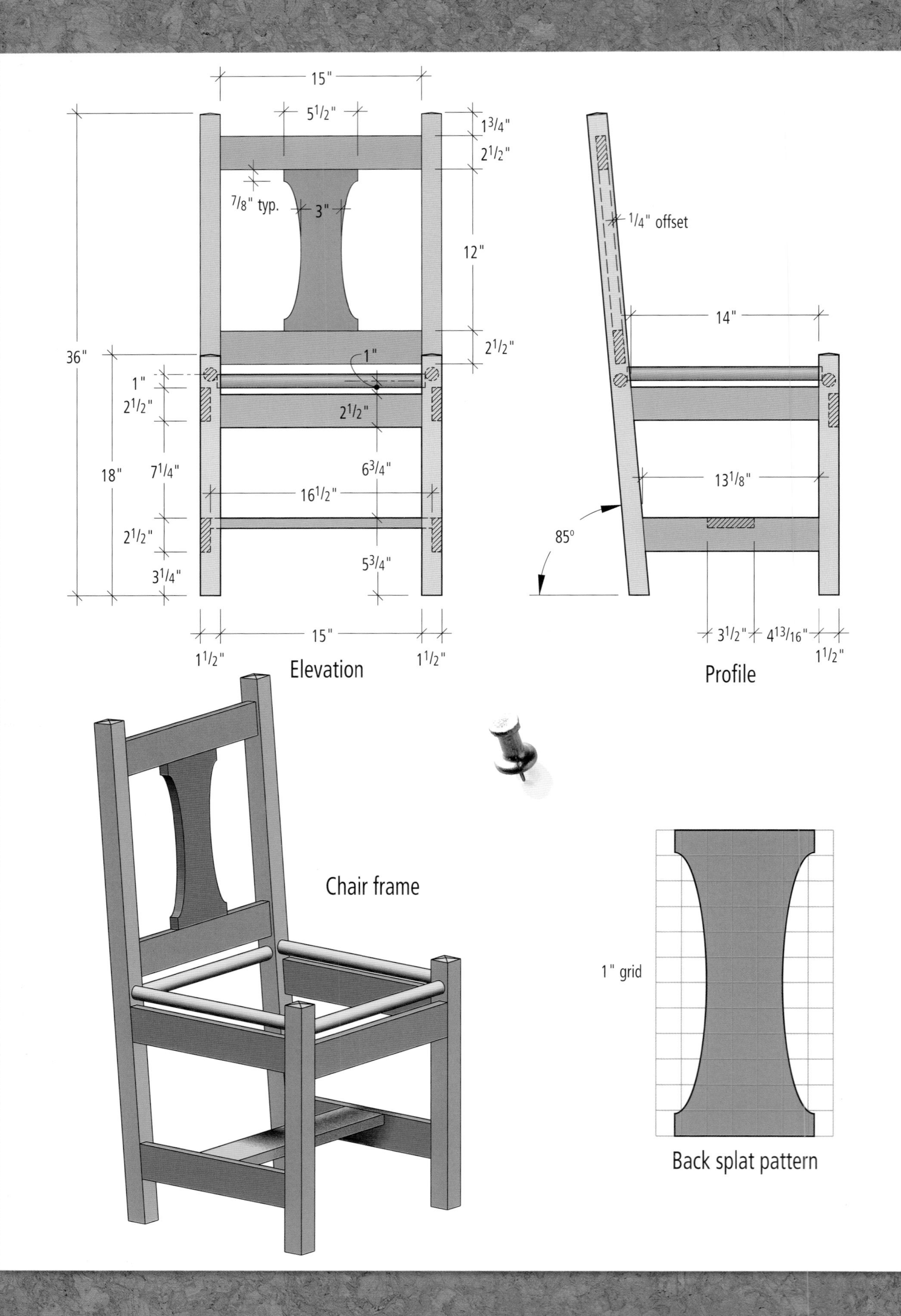
15"
5 1/2"
1 3/4"
2 1/2"
7/8" typ.
3"
12"
36"
2 1/2"
1"
1"
2 1/2"
2 1/2"
18"
7 1/4"
6 3/4"
16 1/2"
2 1/2"
3 1/4"
5 3/4"
15"
1 1/2"
1 1/2"
Elevation
1/4" offset
14"
13 1/8"
85°
3 1/2"
4 13/16"
1 1/2"
Profile
Chair frame
1" grid
Back splat pattern

The dowel holes are offset from one another by 1/2". Make sure you've marked the front and left, or right face of each to avoid drilling the wrong hole in the wrong face. The depth of the hole isn't critical, but I tend to drill till the top of the cutting faces reaches the top of the hole. This is usually about 1/2" deep with most Forstner bits. To keep the hole perpendicular to the leg face, you can stand a try square next to your drill to give you a true 90° angle to follow.

Laying the pieces for the side assemblies on your bench and marking everything will make sure you cut the pockets in the right places. Pencil lines are much easier to sand off than holes in the wrong location.

is straight. I wouldn't want to spend much time sitting with that posture, it's unnatural. So, we need to add angle to the chair. Most times to add angle to the chair you need to bend the back legs. We aren't going to do that.

So how do you create a comfortable angle using straight stock? Easy, tilt the leg. At the miter saw, again with the angle set to 5°, cut the bottom of each back leg. Take as little material as possible in making this cut. You are not looking to shorten the legs, just add the angle.

Hold That Seat, Please

In any chair the longevity of the chair depends on keeping the parts together. A lot of times you can find chairs where the seat is actually holding the parts in place. That is what this chair does.

The seat is wrapped around dowels that are positioned just above the stretchers and slightly offset from one another. Select the front face of the chair legs and mark the side and front edges. Locate the position of the holes and drill them into the front legs only.

To find the dowel positions, start from the pyramid cut and move down 1 1/2" for the center of the side dowel location. Slide down another 1/2" for the location of the front dowel hole.

Make these holes with a drill and 1" Forstner bit, squaring the bit to the stock from both directions. Cut the hole about 1/2" deep – it's not critical because you'll take an exact measurement after the chair is assembled.

Assembling the chair starts with the side profile. Lay the legs of one side of the chair on your bench. Orient the pieces so the angle cut on the back leg is parallel to the edge of the bench. Next, cut the rails for the sides. One end of each piece is cut square while the opposite end is cut at that five degree angle. Both cuts are made at the miter saw.

Fit the rails into position with the legs as shown (next page top left photo). Notice that the front leg (at the left in the photo) is positioned with the front dowel hole facing upward. The top side rails will fit 1/2" below the bottom edge of the side dowel hole or 1" from its center point.

PARTS LIST

			THICKNESS X WIDTH X LENGTH	
NO.	PART	STOCK	INCHES	MILLIMETERS
2	back legs	oak	1 1/2 × 1 1/2 × 36	38 × 38 × 914
2	front legs	oak	1 1/2 × 1 1/2 × 18	38 × 38 × 457
1	front rail	oak	3/4 × 2 1/2 × 15	19 × 64 × 381
2	back splat rails	oak	3/4 × 2 1/2 × 15	19 × 64 × 381
1	back splat	oak	3/4 × 5 1/2 × 12	19 × 140 × 305
2	top side rails	oak	3/4 × 2 1/2 × 14	19 × 64 × 356
2	lower side rails	oak	3/4 × 2 1/2 × 13 1/8	19 × 64 × 333
1	bottom stretcher	oak	3/4 × 3 1/2 × 16 1/2	19 × 89 × 419
4	seat dowels	oak	1 × 15 dia.	25 × 381 dia.

The "clamp-included" pocket hole jig (right) makes cutting twin holes on the ends of all the stretchers much easier. Once the holes are cut, lay the pieces on your bench, square things up and add the screws.

Position the lower side rail starting $3^1/_4$" up from the bottom of the leg. Mark an X at each end of the rails to indicate the area for the pocket screws.

Quick, Strong Connections

Use the pocket-screw jig to cut the holes in the side rails. Make sure that the ends of the rails fit tightly to the base of the jig; the angled cut will tip the rails to one side.

Place the holes, two per end, about $^3/_4$" in from the edges of the rails. Using a framing square will ensure that the chair sides are square to the floor. Position the pieces to the legs as before and make sure that the bottom ends of the legs fit to the square and all faces are tight to the bench. Drive the screws to assemble the sides.

With the side assembly sitting on it's face on the bench, the front rail is screwed into position $^1/_2$" below the dowel hole.

Repeat the same steps for the second side, but this time the chair back or angle must face the opposite direction.

Because the angle is in the side assembly, installing the front rail is a snap. The ends are square-cut straight from the miter saw and the pocket-screw holes are drilled just as they were for the side rails.

Set the side assembly onto the front leg front face down to the bench. Position the front rail $^1/_2$" below the bottom edge of the dowel hole. Hold the face of the rail flat to the bench and drive the screws to attach the front rail. Repeat the steps to attach the second side assembly to the front rail.

Adding a Bit of Design

To add a few shadow lines to the chair back you'll need to set the rails by spacing them off of the front edge of the legs. To make it easy slide a scrap piece of $^1/_4$" plywood, or something else of a consistent thickness, under the rails before adding the screws.

You'll find that the chair is starting to gain in weight, so holding the pieces as you assemble the back is a bit of a task. To make it easier hang the seat portion off the edge of the bench and clamp the top portion of the back leg to your bench. Locate the rails according to the plan, add the spacers under the screw area to create the shadow and drive the screws to attach the back rails.

Once the chair is assembled you need to take an accurate measurement of the stretcher and fit it to the chair. It doesn't fit between two legs so the size will be different.

If you install the stretcher it will get in the way of other operations, but clamping it in place will add strength for the next step.

The side dowel is installed in a hole in the back leg that is drilled at an angle. That hole is parallel to the side rail and is set 1⁄2" above that rail and centered in the leg.

Chuck the 1" forstner bit into the drill and set the center point of the bit in position. Drill the hole to a depth of 1⁄2" while remaining parallel to the rail and square to the leg.

Measure the length of the dowels by placing rulers into the holes as shown in the photo (bottom right). This measurement is exact for that particular dowel location and can vary depending on the depth you drilled the hole. So, each length needs to be measured. Cut the dowels at the miter saw to guarantee a square end.

There is no possible way to install the dowels in the assembled chair without

With the front faces of the rear legs clamped to the bench and the lower part of the chair hanging over the edge, it's time to add the back rails. To add some visual interest to the back, I used some scrap wood to hold the rails back from the front edge of the legs as I added the screws.

The dowel holes in the rear legs need to be drilled parallel to the side stretcher, not perpendicular to the rear leg, otherwise they just won't fit.

By using two steel rules in tandem I'm able to measure the actual required length of the dowels by measuring to the bottom of the dowel holes.

After marking the required length of the splat at the chair itself (above), use a home-made trammel to mark the curves to shape the splat (right).

releasing the hold of the screws. Work one dowel at a time and when the piece is placed in the holes reattach the screws before moving to the next dowel. Also remember to install the stretcher at this time.

Another Shot at Design

The chair back splat is another area where you can influence the overall look of the chair. You can design something fantastic or simply leave it straight. I chose a simple arced cut.

To develop any design, first you need to find the length of the splat. This could be determined while installing the back splat rails or just find the measurement at this time.

Don't rely on rulers or measuring tapes for this. You want a snug fit. Lay the chair on its back then square cut one end of the splat stock. Raise the back off of the bench and slide the splat into position, keeping the square end tight to the lower rail. With a sharp pencil trace the intersection of the splat with the top rail. This is the exact measurement of the splat. Make the next cut at the miter saw.

To draw the arcs you'll need a compass that will expand to a radius of $10\frac{3}{4}$". That's not your average compass! So, you'll have to make your own. Use a piece of scrap or an older (read as not your every day ruler) ruler. Drill a small hole at one end of the piece just big enough for a small finish nail. In fact, I often use the exact nail for this step.

Next, move up the piece to the $10\frac{3}{4}$" line and drill a second hole for the pencil lead to go through. That's your compass a.k.a. a trammel.

Place a scrap of equal thickness perpendicular to the splat material as shown in the photo (above). Measure down $9\frac{1}{2}$" from the intersection of the two pieces and place the nail. This is the pivot point of the compass. As you draw the line you will see that the arc starts about an inch from the end of the splat on all sides. Repeat the steps for the second side of the splat and you are ready to cut those with the jigsaw. Clean up any cut marks with a rasp and sandpaper.

Use the pocket screw as the connection of the splat to the rails. Position clamps over the two pieces, on the face of each

With the splat held flush to the back face of the legs, the pocket screws are driven home, finishing the assembly of your stylin' chair.

Finish the chair before weaving the seat. See the illustration below for weaving details.

piece to keep them aligned as you drive the screws.

Fill any screw holes with the available plugs. This includes all holes in the back and the holes in the side lower rails. Other holes will not be seen once the seat is finished.

Add glue to the hole and tap the plug into place. Allow the fill to dry before sanding smooth.

Adding the Color

The chair is finished with the same formula as the coffee table in this book. Rag on a coat of Olympic Special Walnut stain that is allowed to soak for five minutes before wiping away any excess.

That is followed by a coat of Watco Danish Oil in the walnut tint. This is also allowed to soak for a short time before wiping the chair clean. Once the oil had dried I elected to spray on a coat of shellac. Shellac can be purchased in a spray can and this will allow better control with all the pieces of the chair.

After applying a single coat of shellac which has dried, knock down any nubs with 400-grit sandpaper and add a coat of paste wax and its on to the seat.

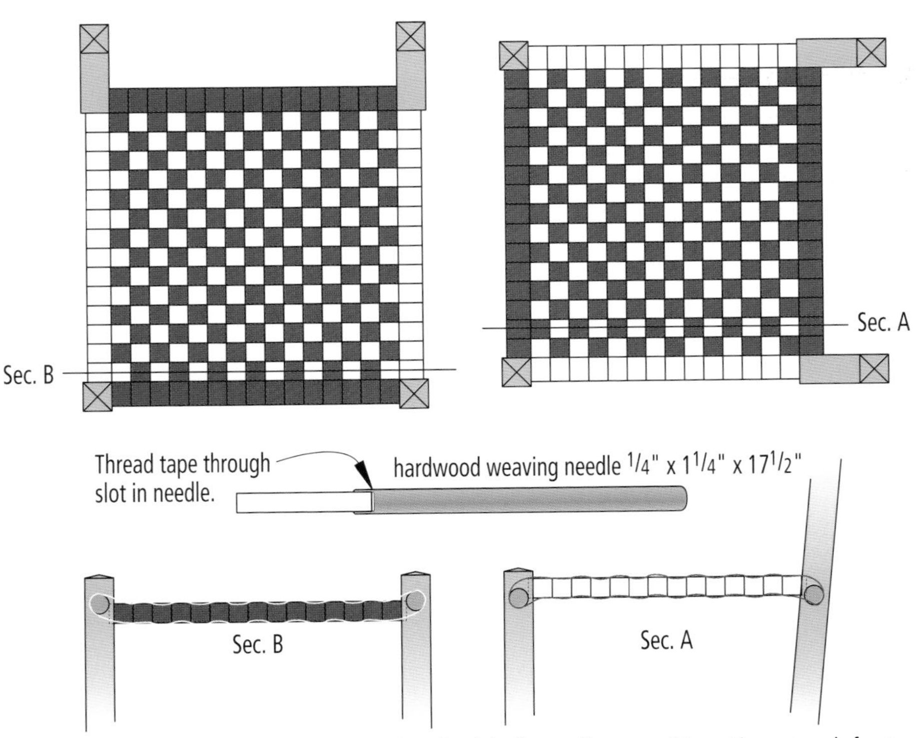

Staple the end of the warp strands to the underside of the front rail to start. Weave these strands front to back between the front and back dowels. Insert a 1"-thick piece of foam between the warp strands. Attach the weave strand to the hardwood needle. Thread the weave strand between the side dowels and between every other warp strand top and bottom. Staple the ends to the underside of the dowels.

SUPPLIERS

ADAMS & KENNEDY — THE WOOD SOURCE
6178 Mitch Owen Rd.
P.O. Box 700
Manotick, ON
Canada K4M 1A6
613-822-6800
www.wood-source.com
Wood supply

ADJUSTABLE CLAMP COMPANY
404 N. Armour St.
Chicago, IL 60622
312-666-0640
www.adjustableclamp.com
Clamps and woodworking tools

B&Q
Portswood House
1 Hampshire Corporate Park
Chandlers Ford
Eastleigh
Hampshire, England SO53 3YX
0845 609 6688
www.diy.com
Woodworking tools, supplies and hardware

BUSY BEE TOOLS
130 Great Gulf Dr.
Concord, ON
Canada L4K 5W1
1-800-461-2879
www.busybeetools.com
Woodworking tools and supplies

CONSTANTINE'S WOOD CENTER OF FLORIDA
1040 E. Oakland Park Blvd.
Fort Lauderdale, FL 33334
800-443-9667
www.constantines.com
Tools, woods, veneers, hardware

FRANK PAXTON LUMBER COMPANY
5701 W. 66th St.
Chicago, IL 60638
800-323-2203
www.paxtonwood.com
Wood, hardware, tools, books

THE HOME DEPOT
2455 Paces Ferry Rd. NW
Atlanta, GA 30339
800-430-3376 (U.S.)
800-628-0525 (Canada)
www.homedepot.com
Woodworking tools, supplies and hardware

KLINGSPOR ABRASIVES INC.
2555 Tate Blvd. SE
Hickory, N.C. 28602
800-645-5555
www.klingspor.com
Sandpaper of all kinds

LEE VALLEY TOOLS LTD.
P.O. Box 1780
Ogdensburg, NY 13669-6780
800-871-8158 (U.S.)
800-267-8767 (Canada)
www.leevalley.com
Woodworking tools and hardware

LOWE'S COMPANIES, INC.
P.O. Box 1111
North Wilkesboro, NC 28656
800-445-6937
www.lowes.com
Woodworking tools, supplies and hardware

MICROPLANE
2401 E. 16th St.
Russellville, AR 72802
800-555-2767
www.us.microplane.com
Rotary shaper and other wood-shaping tools

REID SUPPLY COMPANY
2265 Black Creek Rd.
Muskegon, MI 49444
800-253-0421
www.reidsupply.com
Jig and fixture knobs and clamps

ROCKLER WOODWORKING AND HARDWARE
4365 Willow Dr.
Medina, MN 55340
800-279-4441
www.rockler.com
Woodworking tools, hardware and books

TOOL TREND LTD.
140 Snow Blvd. Unit 1
Concord, ON
Canada L4K 4C1
416-663-8665
Woodworking tools and hardware

TREND MACHINERY & CUTTING TOOLS LTD.
Odhams Trading Estate
St. Albans Rd.
Watford
Hertfordshire, U.K.
WD24 7TR
01923 224657
www.trendmachinery.co.uk
Woodworking tools and hardware

VAUGHAN & BUSHNELL MFG. CO.
P. O. Box 390
Hebron, IL 60034
815-648-2446
www.vaughanmfg.com
Hammers and other tools

WATERLOX COATINGS
908 Meech Ave.
Cleveland, OH 44105
800-321-0377
www.waterlox.com
Finishing supplies

WOODCRAFT SUPPLY LLC
1177 Rosemar Rd.
P.O. Box 1686
Parkersburg, WV 26102
800-535-4482
www.woodcraft.com
Woodworking hardware

WOODWORKER'S HARDWARE
P.O. Box 180
Sauk Rapids, MN 56379-0180
800-383-0130
www.wwhardware.com
Woodworking hardware

WOODWORKER'S SUPPLY
1108 N. Glenn Rd.
Casper, WY 82601
800-645-9292
http://woodworker.com
Woodworking tools and accessories, finishing supplies, books and plans

INDEX

MORE GREAT TITLES FROM POPULAR WOODWORKING!

THE COMPLETE CABINETMAKER'S REFERENCE

By Jeffrey Piontkowski

This indispensable resource for cabinetmakers includes cutting and assembly instructions, along with lists of types and quantities of materials needed for all standard-sized cabinets. You'll also learn how to adapt the projects to build custom-sized pieces.

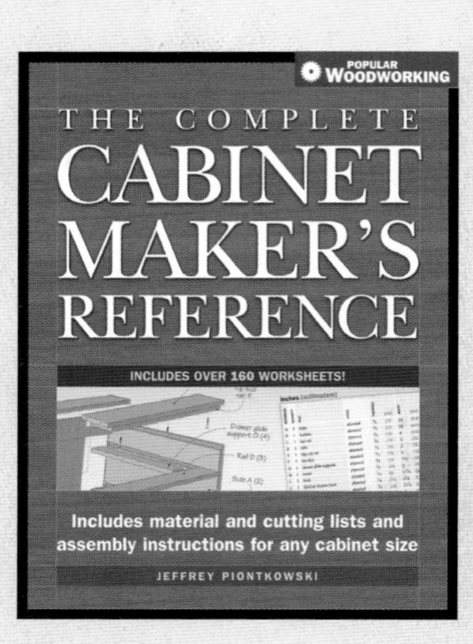

ISBN 13: 978-1-55870-757-3
ISBN 10: 1-55870-757-3,
hc w/ concealed wire-o, 128 p., #70710

ISBN 13: 978-1-55870-774-0
ISBN 10: 1-55870-774-3,
hc w/ concealed wire-o, 144 p., # 70725

BOX BY BOX

By Jim Stack

Hone your woodworking skills one box at a time. In the pages of this book you'll find plans for 21 delightful boxes along with step-by-step instructions for making them. The projects include basic boxes that a novice can make with just a few hand tools to projects that will provide experienced woodworkers with an exciting challenge.

GLEN HUEY'S ILLUSTRATED GUIDE TO BUILDING PERIOD FURNITURE

By Glen Huey

Woodworkers will learn to build their own high-end period furniture with clear, concise instructions, step-by-step photos and a bonus DVD ROM of real-time demonstrations and printable plans.

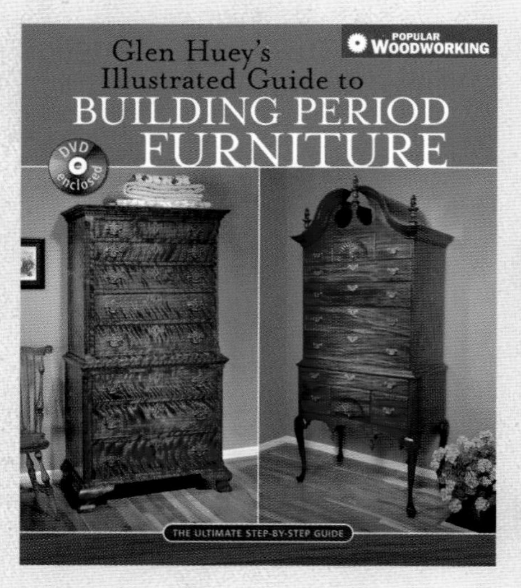

ISBN 13: 978-1-55870-770-2
ISBN 10: 1-55870-770-0,
hc w/ concealed wire-o, 128 p., #70722

ISBN 13: 978-1-55870-784-9
ISBN 10: 1-55870-784-0,
pb, 128 p., # Z0348

WOODSHOP STORAGE SOLUTIONS

By Ralph Laughton

Are you constantly looking for better and more efficient ways of storing and using your tools? This book contains 16 ingenious projects that will make your woodshop totally efficient, extremely flexible and very safe. Projects include: downdraft table, clamp rack, mobile table saw stand, router trolley, router table and more.

These and other great woodworking books are available at your local bookstore, woodworking stores, or from online suppliers.

www.popularwoodworking.com